THE AMERICAN INDIANS

T0370619

Chippewa Chief

THE AMERICAN INDIANS

NORTH OF MEXICO

BY

W. H. MINER

Member of the American Anthropological Association

Cambridge :

at the University Press

1917

CAMBRIDGE
UNIVERSITY PRESS

University Printing House, Cambridge CB2 8BS, United Kingdom

Cambridge University Press is part of the University of Cambridge.

It furthers the University's mission by disseminating knowledge in the pursuit of education, learning and research at the highest international levels of excellence.

www.cambridge.org
Information on this title: www.cambridge.org/9781107456471

© Cambridge University Press 1917

First published 1917
First paperback edition 2014

A catalogue record for this publication is available from the British Library

ISBN 978-1-107-45647-1 Paperback

TO

WOODROW WILSON
PRESIDENT OF THE UNITED STATES

PREFACE

THERE are two reasons for offering this little volume on the Indians of North America, north of the Mexican border. At present there is not before the public a readable, comprehensive or authentic account of the original inhabitants of the American continent, which may in any way be termed popular. Monographs of varying excellence have appeared, covering many phases of the subject, as well as numerous extensive and learned treatises bearing upon nearly all branches of American ethnology, but, with the exception of several indifferent attempts at historical writing and one or two elementary works, there is nothing that can be referred to as desirable or satisfactory to the general reader. It is not, however, a dearth of material that confronts the student but rather a want of systematic arrangement which has heretofore been lacking; this want, it is hoped, may, in part at least, be supplied by this volume.

In the second place, it is readily to be remarked that interest in the study, both cultural and descriptive, of this branch of the world's family, is, particularly in America, constantly increasing. As the original data disappear, so do new generations realise the value of what has passed, and every portion of history or folklore thus preserved and studied becomes to the highest degree valuable and interesting.

Many Americans of to-day, especially those of the middle and far west, may be direct descendants of those hardy pioneers or frontiersmen who were, but a few years since, either friends or foes of the original inhabitants of the lands they now occupy. These or like instances are, for the most part, well within the memory of the living, and this interest, already well advanced, will continually develop.

Obviously, what is included within the scope of the present work can be little more than an introductory sketch. What has of necessity been omitted would readily fill many larger volumes. On the other hand, if it induces the reader to follow the subject at greater length, it will have achieved the aim of many efforts of a more elaborate nature.

The special work in this particular field now being carried on enthusiastically and with thoroughness by the Bureau of American Ethnology and the Carnegie Institution in Washington, the Field-Columbian Museum of Chicago, the Peabody Museum of Harvard University, the American Museum of Natural History, in New York, and many of the research and historical departments of the larger American Universities, as well as numerous American Historical Societies, is of inestimable value to the future historian of the American aborigines, and must under no circumstances be overlooked. To make acknowledgement even remotely here to those to whom I am indebted for assistance, would be quite impossible. The bibliography included as an appendix is the best possible form wherein to denote those who have indirectly helped.

I wish at this time especially to express my gratitude to Mr F. W. Hodge of the Bureau of American Ethnology, who has always held himself in readiness to assist, and who, as editor of that encyclopaedic work, *Handbook of North American Indians*, has done more to present a clear understanding of the first Americans than has any other among present-day ethnologists. To Dr Peter Giles, Master of Emmanuel College, Cambridge, my sincere thanks are due for careful supervision of the proof and much valuable assistance and advice.

W. H. M.

"RESTHOLME,"
CEDAR RAPIDS,
IOWA, U.S.A.
October 12, 1916.

CONTENTS

CHAPTER I

INTRODUCTION

To obtain even a cursory knowledge of the native races of the North American continent a general idea of the country in which this branch of mankind is autochthonous is wholly essential.

Under the general term Indian, many who are not students of anthropology or allied sciences are apt to confuse not only the inhabitants of North, Central and South America, but also the northern tribes of the Canadian arctic region, as well as those of Mexico. To a great extent this definition is correct, yet the differences are in many instances so great, for example, between the short, heavy set Eskimo of the north and the tall, slender men of the Tīmūcuañ or Karankawan families of the Gulf of Mexico, that it may seem at times difficult to reconcile many facts as we understand them.

It is well therefore, in approaching the subject, tc define briefly the general characteristics of the countries now designated as the

United States and the Dominion of Canada and to outline briefly not only the reason for the apparent diversity of races on the continent but also the method by which the study of the original inhabitants is now being pursued, as well as the causes or reasons that have led to this form of procedure.

Considering that portion of the North American continent lying from 29° N. to the Arctic Circle, we find included the whole of Canada and the greater portion of the United States. This space, therefore, is ample for the purpose of studying climatic environment and it will be readily appreciated that such an area can produce marked racial groupings. Thus the physiographic features of the country are of interest and especially do these assist in deducing many facts which have to do with migrations, while again they suggest various reasons for the preference of Indian tribes for certain localities, as the desirability of mountain, plain or woodland according to choice.

The matter of the coastal formation of a country is of prime importance. It means much to an invader and but little less to the colonist, hence it is indirectly a matter of close affiliation in the study of the Indian. The American coasts, both Atlantic and Pacific, are uneven, often, in the case of the former, rugged in the extreme; good harbours with accompanying peninsulas are frequent, and according to excellent authorities, the discovery as well as rapid growth of the early colonies such as Virginia (originally including the whole of New England) and the other Atlantic seaboard sections preceded similar action on the western ocean.

From the great bodies of water that surround a continent, it is natural to consider the drainage system, and in this feature America is in no way deficient. The larger part of the great interior basin, known as the Mississippi Valley, is given outlet largely through the river of that name or by its numerous tributaries, the Arkansas, Red, Missouri and Ohio, or through the Great Lakes and the St Lawrence. This valley extends from the Gulf of Mexico far into the arctic region, in which latter section it is drained by the Mackenzie river into the Arctic Ocean and, principally, by the Nelson river into Hudson Bay. Along the east coast numerous smaller streams, as the Connecticut, Hudson, Delaware, Potomac, etc., act in a similar manner and with the Yadkin, Catawba and Savannah, extend nearly to the extreme south; the south-eastern low country being drained into the Gulf of Mexico by the Apalachicola and minor streams which join the Mississippi in its lower course.

The far west has its own so-called watershed running without regular course through the Rocky Mountain chain, to the west of which all drainage is to the Pacific with few exceptions. The foremost streams of this section are the Yukon flowing into the Behring Sea, the Fraser and Columbia into the Pacific, and the Colorado river of the west which empties into the Gulf of California.

These systems of waterways exertèd a considerable influence on the habitat of the American Indian and next, indeed if not of equal importance, for varying reasons, are the highlands or mountain ranges. As means of modifying conditions of climate or acting as impedimenta to the advance or spread of peoples the great mountain ranges should be carefully considered. Three systems are in North America and may be thought of in the order here noted. First, the Cordilleras, an extraordinary chain extending along the whole western section of the country from Alaska to Central America. These in fact comprise a vast plateau with an average breadth of nearly one thousand miles in

parts of the United States and with an eleva-
tion of from 5000 to 10,000 feet, from the base
of which rise numerous mountain ranges extending in a direction generally north and south and
variously designated as the Rocky Mountains,
the Sierra Nevada, and the Cascade Range of
Oregon, Washington and the Canadian North-
west. Among these is to be found the highest
peak on the continent, Mt McKinley, rising to an
altitude of 20,464 feet. Second, the Coast Range
is to the extreme west.

Toward the Atlantic and across the great
central basin, is the eastern or Appalachian
System, attaining no great height at any point
yet filled with tradition as having borne a most
important part in the country's history. Extending from eastern Canada south-westerly
along the Atlantic coast to Georgia, it in
no way presents a continuous range, though
usually so regarded. There are divisions of
various groups such as the Black, Green, White,
Catskills, etc., not to forget the historically
important Blue Ridge which forms the eastern
boundary of a comparatively narrow plateau of
from 25 to 200 miles in width, the central portion
of which is relatively low land broken occasionally by intersecting lines of hills and extending

roughly from the borders of Pennsylvania and New Jersey to the Gulf States. This area early became designated as "The Valley" or "The Valley of Virginia."

If it be possible to form in the mind's eye a relief map of the continent, it is readily seen that the predominance of high altitude is almost wholly in the extreme west. Thus beginning with the Coast Range, the slope of which practically reaches the Pacific, there may be mentioned in their proper order the Cascade and Sierra Nevada Mountains, a continuous range from upper Canada through Mexico; from Canada again the Bitter Root Mountains, continuing southerly as the Rockies, the latter made up of numerous smaller ranges, as the Big Horn, Wasatch, Black Hills, Uintah, etc.; a range (the Laurentian), attaining no great height, arises in north-central Labrador and runs south by west until it diminishes at a point between Hudson Bay and the Great Lakes, and finally the Appalachians, beginning in Nova Scotia, terminate in Alabama. Thus by keeping in view these physiographic features a clearer idea of the country originally occupied by the Indian races of the greater part of North America can be attained.

Another striking peculiarity and one of great importance is that most remarkable chain of lakes in both the British and American possessions. These marvellous fresh water seas cover a vast area of middle eastern America and are supplemented in the Canadian North-west by the Great Bear, Great Slave and Athabasca Lakes, acting as a northern continuation of the first group almost to the Arctic Ocean, as well as Lakes Manitoba, Winnipeg and Lake of the Woods, emptying into Hudson Bay. In Utah, also, is the Great Salt Lake with no discernible outlet.

The region of the Prairies or Plains extends roughly from the Rocky Mountains due east, and well into the State of Ohio, though seen at its best in the mid-western States of Illinois, Indiana and Iowa. These prairies are not, as many erroneously conceive, a vast expanse of unbroken or level country, but are often rolling, even hilly, and in parts intersected by streams large and small which break the monotony of almost limitless unwooded tracts.

The great desert region of the United States occupies a section situate for the most part between the Rocky Mountains and the Sierra Nevada Range, including therefore the greater part of the State of Nevada, portions of Utah and Arizona and of southern California, and through this arid country the Colorado, the only important river draining the section, flows into the Gulf of California. Lying between the mountain systems of the Pacific coast are numerous valleys, distinctive among which are the lowlands surrounding Puget Sound in Washington and the Willamette country in Oregon.

The preceding gives a somewhat hasty *résumé* of the general features of the North American continent north of the Mexican border. It will in part help in what may follow, by assisting somewhat toward an understanding of racial distribution as well as a clearer idea of cultural characteristics. A great deal may be gleaned from the geologist and mineralogist, and indeed from the archaeologist, though in reality the geological record is a simple one. It is generally conceded that the oldest part of America is the Laurentian plateau in eastern Canada and from this point progress was made toward the west. The Cordilleras are believed to be comparatively recent, showing evidences of late volcanic eruption. Mexican volcanoes still exist and even in Alaska they are not wholly extinct. Geology proves the existence of a great glacial sheet of comparatively recent occurrence covering a part

of the United States and nearly the whole of
Canada, as its area is readily marked by the various
lakes and watercourses throughout the divided
region. After it receded came the great drift of rich
soil known as the prairies at a later period. Its
action therefore became of the utmost importance.

It will be readily seen that the land as finally
inhabited by the Americans of a prehistoric era
was one rich in variety of natural advantages and
that its adaptability was merely a matter of time
and opportunity. How it became peopled and
by whom is still, even to our foremost ethnologists, a matter of more or less conjecture and the
origin of the Indian will be discussed in as sane
and impartial a manner as possible in the following chapter.

The theory that man originated in America
has long been abandoned. The absence from the
continent of anthropoid apes proves such an
idea untenable; hence the population must have
come from the Old World. In his new home in
America environment unquestionably brought
about change in habit and custom. Extremes
of climate to be had between the Arctic Circle
and the Tropic of Cancer naturally led to various
conditions of life, social, economic and in-
dustrial, yet ethnologists agree as to a similarity

of type. Furthermore the Indian races of North America, while differing largely in habitat, and influenced by conditions of life and place, as well as climate, are distinctly one race throughout.

The Indian of the mountains differed slightly in his manner of living from his brethren of the plains, as did the woodland Indian of Canada for instance from those of the Pueblos of Arizona. These last in turn had not such familiarity with the lakes and rivers as had the inhabitants of the country to the north-west; hence an understanding of the physical features as a help toward historical sequence.

It is usually difficult to formulate a scheme for practical study of the native races of America. The present-day anthropologist sets about this by distinguishing groups through one of four sets of characteristics; geographical, physical, general culture and linguistic. It is by the linguistic method that such work will continue, as it is in this way that the best results have generally been attained. While there is no scheme of classification accepted by all students, unity is always recognised through the linguistic diversity, and it is a most remarkable feature of American ethnology to-day that authorities admit either fifty-six or fifty-eight distinct linguistic families or stocks among the Indians north of Mexico, more than one-third of the number being found in what are now the States of Oregon and California on the Pacific coast.

To conclude therefore, the study of the American Indian is based primarily on linguistics. He is judged in a secondary way by his habitat and the manners and customs as gathered from his family or tribal relations, and finally from the standpoint of anthropometry. All of these features will be elucidated in what follows.

CHAPTER II

In his first letter dated (February) 1493, Columbus makes the earliest mention of the American Indians under such a name. The discovery of a new continent by the Genoese opened to the world a wonderful new field for speculation, though it was thought to have been none other than a portion of India thus reached by a new route. Hence the cognomen *Indio* of the Spaniard, Portuguese and Italian; *Indien* of the Frenchman; *Indianer* of the German, etc.

As to the probable origin of this race of mankind, it is quite impossible, even at the present stage of ethnological investigation, to arrive at any definite conclusion, though it is to be confessed that at the close of the nineteenth century numerous rational hypotheses had been advanced but very various in character. To take up the subject in proper sequence it may be stated that inasmuch as none of the early Hebrew traditions mentioned the American people, the Spaniards until the time of Las Casas arrived at the

conclusion that they could not be properly regarded as men similar to those referred to in the
Biblical accounts, a view which was eventually
counteracted by a papal bull from Rome. When
it was discovered that the Indian might be considered human and in consequence worthy of some
consideration, efforts tending toward the discovery
of his origin thenceforth became matters of interest
among scholars of various schools, and the conclusions drawn were in many instances remarkable.

Gomara, Lerius and even Lescabot held that
the Indians descended from the Canaanites who
were driven abroad by Joshua, and the theory
accepted by the great majority was to the effect
that they were the lost tribes of Israel.

One early writer propounded an artful theory
that they were descendants from Asiatics with
Magog, the second son of Japhet, as the head,
and numerous other tales, some even less likely
or ingenious, were among the earliest.

Within the last quarter of a century, or indeed,
within the last decade, our knowledge of the subject has assumed something of cogent shape and
it is thought but a few years will have passed
before definite facts can be handled and absolute
decisions rendered as to first man in America.

A great abundance of literature has been

produced on the subject since Humboldt in 1810 ventured his opinions. Students of high standing wrote on the perplexing question and some with Lord Kames in the eighteenth century, and much later Morton, and Nott and Gliddon professed the belief that the Indian was autochthonous. Grotius writes of the early Christian Ethiopians, who he tells us first peopled Yucatan. That the ancestors of the Americans came by way of the Pacific Ocean and in part from north-eastern Asia is the theory held by Mitchell. McCullogh, as early as 1829, felt confident that at an early period America had been connected with a lost land from the west, over which was "allowed a free transit for quadrupeds," and his idea of a lost Atlantis is by no means dormant at the present time.

Quatrefages, reviewing the subject carefully as late as 1887, concludes the Indians to be a conglomerate race, composed in part of Polynesians and others of the South Seas, while Pickering believed in an origin partly Mongolian and partly Malay. The general consensus of opinion during the last century is to the effect that, with the exception of the Eskimo, the natives of America are wholly of one race and descendants from early immigrants from north-eastern Asia, and especially of Mongolian stock.

It is to be remarked, however, that the most recent writers generally agree that America was peopled first by some form of immigration and secondly by local multiplication, but as to the locality as well as the nature and period of such a movement there is yet animated discussion. J. Kollmann thinks that a race of pygmies preceded the Indians, and Ameghino believes not only the American race but mankind in general originated in South America; indeed the antiquity of man on the American continent has given rise to various problems which are, at this time, receiving an unusual amount of attention from the scientific world.

As the natives were wholly without a system of writing, or at least did not transmit any such tangible records, the knowledge of what may have occurred previous to the Columbian discovery is obviously supplied only by tradition or the more or less slight records of archaeologic or ethnologic phenomena.

The potent physical characteristics of the whole American race, from Alaska to the southern extreme of South America, seem to indicate clearly an absolute separation from parental stock. The existence of various culture groups, wholly distinct as to religion or aesthetics, social customs and technology, would presume a somewhat exclusive life in certain independent areas. There is, unfortunately, but a vague record even among the most advanced tribes that proves of service in ascertaining the time periods of occupancy of the continent by the race, or even in tracing more recent events. It is practically impossible to write with assurance of any but recent centuries, yet with the aid of biology and geology, archaeology has supplied data of the greatest value, though many weighty problems will indefinitely remain unsolved. It was ultimately concluded that the course of primitive history had been the same in both the northern and southern continents, but even here the final decision has not been reached. Attempts to establish a chronology have failed thus far.

Interesting have been the claims set forth for glacial man, notably the finding of a portion of a human femur said to show glacial striae and traces of human workmanship found at a depth of twenty-one feet. On this last single object the claim for glacial antiquity in the Delaware region exists. Other finds east of the Alleghanies lack scientific verification, though Ohio has reported articles of human workmanship of the glacial period, and in the west, particularly at

Little Falls, Minnesota, artificial objects of quartz have been found in flood-plain deposits of gravel and sand. Winchell believes this flood-plain to have been finally abandoned by the Mississippi river about the period of the close of the glacial epoch in the valley; yet this leads to no definite conclusion. Curious finds such as the "Lansing Man," the "Nampa Image" and the "Calaveras Man" are of possible importance but unfortunately inconclusive.

As previously mentioned, the study of the North American Indian is based to a great extent upon linguistic classification, and the diversity of language is one of the most extraordinary features in American ethnology. This phenomenon was noticed by numerous early explorers in the field of American philology, but it was not until 1836 that the first purely scientific treatise appeared in Gallatin's *Synopsis of the Indian Tribes within the United States*, etc., published by the American Antiquarian Society. This book easily marks an era in American linguistic science, inasmuch as the writer introduced comparative methods and showed in detail the boundaries of various families. The work may in fact be taken as a starting point, since nothing of moment exists of anterior date covering the subject of the systematic philology of North America. Powell's *Indian Linguistic Families of America north of Mexico*, published in 1891, is a monument of its kind and is now in course of revision by Boas and others. In the list of families which follows, the last-named authority has been adopted, as recent investigation shows the probability as well as possibility of incorporating under single linguistic heads several heretofore supposedly distinct stocks. To be exact, the literature referring to these various stocks is in no wise uniform :

List of linguistic families of the American Indians, north of Mexico (after Boas).

1. Eskimo (arctic coast).
2. Athapascan (north-western interior, Oregon, California, south-west).
3. Tlingit (coast of southern Alaska).
4. Haida (Queen Charlotte Islands, British Columbia).
5. Salishan (southern British Columbia and northern Washington).
6. Chemakum (west coast of Washington).
7. Wakashan (Vancouver Island).
8. Algonquian (region south of Hudson Bay and eastern Woodlands).
9. Beothuk (Newfoundland).
10. Tsimshian (northern coast of British Columbia).
11. Siouan (northern plains west of Mississippi and North Carolina).
12. Iroquoian (lower Great Lakes and North Carolina).

13. Caddoan (southern part of plains west of Mississippi).
14. Muskhogean (south-eastern United States).
15. Kiowa (middle western plains).
16. Shoshonean (western plateaus of United States).
17. Kutenai (south-eastern interior of British Columbia).
18. Pima (Arizona and Sonora).
19. Yuma (Arizona and lower California).
20. Chinook (lower Columbia river).
21. Yakona (Yaquina bay).
22. Kus (coast of central Oregon).
23. Takelma (Rogue river, Oregon).
24. Kalapuya (Willamette valley, Oregon).
25. Waiilaptuan (Cascade range east of Willamette, Oregon).
26. Klamath (south-eastern interior of Oregon).
27. Sahaptin (interior of Oregon).
28. Quoratean (Klamath river).
29. Weitspekan (lower Klamath river).
30. Shasta (north-east interior of California).
31. Wishok (north coast of California).
32. Yana (eastern tributaries of upper Sacramento river, California).
33. Chimarico (head waters of Sacramento river, California).
34. Wintun (valley of Sacramento river).
35. Maidu (east of Sacramento river).
36. Yuki (north of Bay of San Francisco).
37. Pomo (coast north of Bay of San Francisco).
38. Washo (Lake Washoe, Nevada, and California).
39. Moquelumnan (east of lower Tulare river, California).
40. Yokuts (southern Tulare river, California).
41. Costanoan (south of Bay of San Francisco, California).
42. Esselenian (coast of southern California).

43. Salinan (coast of southern California).
44. Chumashan (coast of southern California).
45. Tanoan (Pueblos of New Mexico and Arizona).
46. Zuni (Pueblos of New Mexico and Arizona).
47. Keres (Pueblos of New Mexico and Arizona).
48. Pakawan (from Cibolo creek, Texas, into the State of Coahuila, Mexico).
49. Karankawa (coast of Gulf of Mexico west of Atakapa).
50. Tonkawa (inland from preceding).
51. Atakapa (coast of Gulf of Mexico west of Chitimacha).
52. Chitimacha (coast of Gulf of Mexico west of Mississippi).
53. Tunica (coast of Gulf of Mexico west of Mississippi).
54. Yuchi (east Georgia).
55. Timuqua (Florida).

This list cannot be claimed as final and, as work progresses, certain modifications will of necessity be incorporated, yet it is an excellent groundwork toward a complete knowledge and the changes made will not be fundamental.

Physically the native North American may be detailed for general understanding as follows. The prevailing colour of the skin is brown, a fact not usually understood or realised, though it may be stated that colour differs to a large extent according to locality, ranging in shade from a whitish-yellow to chocolate. The hair is almost always black and straight, the beard scanty, especially on the sides of the face, and as a rule,

Principal
Linguistic Families
of
AMERICAN INDIANS
NORTH OF MEXICO

hair is lacking entirely on the body. Compared
with white men or women the head is smaller
on an average, as is the brain cavity. Mental
characteristics are similar throughout various
tribes and the heart beat is slow. There is no
distinct skin odour.

A study of the eyes reveals a more or less
uniform shade of dark brown with conjunctiva of
yellowish-white, and there is a tendency prevalent among certain tribes toward an upward
slant of the eye slit. Prognathism, at least to
a medium degree, is noticeable in the lower face,
while the mouth is usually of fair size with lips
a trifle more full than in whites, and the bridge of
the nose especially in men is well developed. Teeth
are generally of medium size and the ears large.

The neck, while of moderate length, is seldom
or never thin, the chest being deeper if anything
than in the average white. As is usual in savage
races, the breasts of the women are conical though
of medium size, and there is a complete absence
of steatopygy. The lower limbs and legs in both
men and women cannot be termed shapely and
the calves are small. The hands and feet are of
medium size.

These data are sufficient for the reader who
does not wish to make a close investigation of the

physical anthropology of the race. The above features are, broadly speaking, possessed by practically all of the Indians occupying the region included in this study. It may be mentioned, however, that the longevity of the Indian is very much the same as that of the healthy white man, though there is usually little decrepitude among the aged.

CHAPTER III

The social status of the Indian as an individual is interesting. To properly understand his code of ethics or to obtain an insight into his manner of life and thought, it becomes necessary to approach through a somewhat tangled maze of what may be termed organisation or consanguinity. Easily the most potent elements in his sociology are the clan and gens, kinship groups within the boundaries of which degrees of relationship between members are totally disregarded, and Hewitt has defined the former most concisely as "an intertribal exogamic group of persons either actually or theoretically consanguine."

Surrounding the origin of these systems discussion has been active for some time and continues unceasingly; furthermore the view was commonly held that the clan was a direct outgrowth from the family. On the other hand many leading ethnologists contend that the family, in the common meaning of the term, is a recent formation within the clan.

This form of organisation is by no means universal among the North American tribes, but where it does exist the distinctive character is clearly defined. Of importance is the fact that lineal descent, inheritance of personal and common property, and the hereditary right to public office or trust are traced only through the female line; indeed, among some tribes consanguine kinship is traced through the blood of the woman only, whereas in the gens, descent is through the male, and membership in the clan or gens constitutes citizenship in the tribe, conferring certain social, political and even religious duties absolutely denied to aliens. Totemism, however, or even the worship of personal totems by individuals or groups is not an essential feature of these bodies.

Although details both various and important are numbered in clan organisation, one alone can be dwelt upon here, namely the law of exogamy. Members of the same group must not marry and for violation of this rule death was the usual punishment. This law is as strongly defined to-day as in the beginning.

Though occasionally so, it is not customary for

names of clans or gentes to be derived directly from common objects, as birds or animals. Generally such names denote some characteristic or favourite haunt, or even some archaic name referring to bird or animal or thing. As an instance of this a certain clan among the Seneca may be noted as being named from the deer *ne'ogĕⁿ'* "cloven foot," while the clan name is *hadinioñgwai'iu'* "those whose nostrils are large and fine looking." On the other hand, among the Iowa the five important gentes are known as the Black Bear, *Tuña*ⁿ-*pⁱⁿ*; Wolf, *Mi-tci'-ra-tce*; Eagle and Thunder, *Tcé-xi-ta*; Elk, *Qó-ta-tci*; and Beaver, *Pá-gça*[1].

The number of clans in different tribes varies; as, for example, the Mohawk and Oneida of Iroquois stock have but three, whereas the Wyandot of the same stock have twelve. Again clans and gentes are generally, though not invariably, subdivided or further organised into phratries or units of organisation for ceremonial and other assemblages and festivals, but as such bodies have no officers. From these divisions are formed the tribes.

A close study of the political arrangement of the numerous divisions would be impossible here. The government of the clan or gens is

[1] See note p. 151.

in part a development of hereditary rights arising
primarily in the family, and the supervision of
the phratry is under the control of the chiefs or
elders serving as directors of the more important
branch. The oversight of a tribe is evolved
through that of the clan, and a confederation
such as the League of the Iroquois is governed
on this principle.

An examination of the tribal organisation of
the North American Indians usually reveals three
divisions, geographic or consanguineal in character, viz. social or governmental classes; chiefs
and councils having particular powers and rights;
and fraternities of a generally semi-religious
character. Further, tribes may be divided
roughly into those possessing but loose organisation, and again those in clearly defined groups
(clans or gentes) who were strictly exogamic.
Among the former may be cited the Eskimo,
among the latter, numerous southern tribes as
the Pueblo, Navaho and many in the Atlantic
and Gulf States. Thus it is to be seen that the
units of political and social life of the native
Americans are (*a*) the family, (*b*) the clan and
gens, (*c*) the phratry, and (*d*) the tribe.

Of these the tribe, if the confederation be
excepted, is the only form completely organised.

As a rule military were carefully discriminated from civil functions. The civil form of government was generally lodged in a chosen body of men called chiefs, and of this office there were several grades. For example, a civil chief was not by virtue of his office a leader in a military way. *Per contra*, a military leader might not be called upon for an opinion in council exercising legislation. Thus in tribal society practically all units have the privilege of holding councils, beginning with the *ohwachira* or kinship group, next the family, followed by the united *ohwachira* councils with their officers, who in turn form the council of the clan or gens. This clan or gens has the right to hold council; the chiefs of the clans or gentes are the tribal chiefs, forming the tribal council; occasions of vast importance demand a grand council composed of chiefs and subchiefs, the matrons, head warriors of the *ohwachira* and leading men of the tribe. There may be also a council of the confederation, where such exists; hence there are found family, clan, gentile, tribal and confederation councils respectively, when essential, each exercising sway in separate and independent jurisdictions and each with its own leader or headman, or chief.

There are varying degrees in the scale of

social life among the Indians as among the white
nations, the greatest development north of
Mexico being without doubt among the Iroquois
of the north-east, as shown by Morgan in *The
League of the Iroquois*. From this there is a drop
to an almost opposite extreme, notably among the
Eskimo or some of the tribes of California, and
Dixon describing the northern Maidu of the
western coast finds no trace of gentile or even
totemic grouping. Coming east again the Seneca
of New York have a written constitution con-
firmed by the legislature of that State.

The home life of the Indian is little understood; yet its importance is manifold, as his
domestic arrangements are more complex than
might be imagined. That there has been little
change in his code of morals or his ethical concepts is proven from the fact that his customs
in this respect are practically the same to-day as
when first known to the white man. Just how
much of these manners or morals has been
absorbed from the outsider is hard to estimate,
and there are still certain tribes which have
repulsed the alien race and remain, if early
testimony can be relied upon, quite unchanged.

To outline the ethics of the primitive peoples
of the American continent would be difficult in

the space allotted. There undoubtedly existed, however, a standard of right and wrong, and from various sources there comes the knowledge of a conscience among the Indians and the fact that it was held in dread. Among all tribes of standing there was the power of public opinion, ofttimes compelling the most refractory. In some cases executive bands had power to punish offenders acting in violation of the orders of the tribal council, yet thus far no evidence of even the rudiments of courts of justice seems available.

The truth was invariably expected of those from whom reports were received concerning any events of importance in affairs of interest to the tribe or council. Inaccurate reporters met with disgrace. The warrior meeting with some signal success could not claim more than his due, and the common punishment for lying was the burning of the liar's tent and property by tribal sanction. A broken promise was equivalent to lying, and instances are not uncommon where Indians have kept their word at the risk of death.

Honesty was taught from infancy, but as war removed all barriers governing ethics, pillage was legitimate. A thieving Indian was not unknown nevertheless, but considered without the pale, as would be true among a white community under similar conditions. A theft being committed, tribal authorities demanded restitution, and flogging as well as social ostracism resulted.

Murder when committed within the tribe was invariably punished either by exile or, in some instances, by allowing the murderer to become an object of vengeance; in a word, truth, honesty and the general safety of human life were universally recognised as matters essential to the welfare and prosperity of the tribe, and their observance was duly enforced.

The penalty for adultery varied among different tribes. Ordinarily the aggrieved party chose his or her own method of punishment.

Witchcraft was a most serious offence and meant death. It was believed that the witch or wizard brought sickness or distemper in one form or another, and, as the easiest method of prevention, the sorcerer was removed immediately. A mistaken code of ethics was in part to blame for this peremptory action and a lack of knowledge of disease quite sufficient to make it final.

The home life of the Indian may be somewhat better understood after this brief survey of some of his more personal modes of thought. His morals, as savage or barbarous morals may be

considered, were far from the lowest order.   His
etiquette and daily ceremonials are noteworthy.

Few of the dwellings of the American Indians,
whatever their form of structure, were visibly
divided, yet for each member of the family a
distinct space was allotted.   His pack and goods
of one kind or another were here in the daytime,
his bed spread in their stead at night.   A guest
space was set apart which was, among the Plains
tribes, at the back facing the entrance.   This
aperture was generally made to open toward
the east.   The guest space was often of the
utmost importance and used not infrequently
either by friend, messenger or perhaps delegate,
as occasion demanded.

Even methods of greeting were studied.   A
familiar friend or acquaintance was spoken to at
once without formality, but should the visitor
come on business his advent was in silence which
remained unbroken for some moments.   On receiving delegations, only the older men of a party
spoke.   Among all tribes undue haste was a
stamp of ill-breeding, and no visitor left the
dwelling of his host without words of parting to
show that his visit was at an end.

Etiquette among many tribes demanded when
a person was addressed that a term of relationship

rather than the proper name be used. Elders
were greeted as grandfather or grandmother, and
titles of this kind were also applied to men or
women of distinction in the tribe. Outsiders
were often accosted as friends, and members of
different clans or gentes were designated as
cousins or "my father's clansman," etc., though
belonging to the same tribe. Among certain
tribes etiquette restricted direct speech between
a woman and her son-in-law and often also
with her father-in-law, according to certain
authorities, while among some tribes the men
and women used different forms of speech and
such a distinction was carefully observed.

That man should precede woman when walk-
ing or in entering a lodge was customary, "to
make the way safe for her," and due respect was
shown to elders both in behaviour and speech.
These and many other details of like character
could be cited at greater length, as for instance
the fact that familiar conversation was at no
time permitted except between relatives, and a
general reserve was usual in the behaviour of men
toward women. There was also a formal manner
observed in both standing and sitting, especially
among the women. The latter stood as a rule
with their feet close together and legs perfectly

straight, and if unencumbered the hands hung down and were advanced somewhat, the fingers being extended and the palms pressed lightly against the dress. As a rule the females sat with one foot beneath them and slightly to one side. The men usually sat cross-legged.

Smoking whether ceremonial or social had its peculiarities, much formality being used both in exchanging materials and in passing and returning the pipe.

The subject of kinship as existing among the Indians is complex and difficult of explanation. Even to touch on it here otherwise than in a most brief manner is impossible, yet it forms ethnologically a fundamental subject. Primarily, that relation existent between two or more persons whose blood is derived from common ancestors forms kinship, which may in turn be lineal or collateral. In referring to an entire body or group of kindred it is essential that some one person be specifically mentioned as a starting point. For general argument every person belongs to two separate families or "kinship groups" which before his or her birth were entirely apart for the purpose of marriage, the inheritance of property as well as other rights, obligations and privileges. In the person of the individual in question these

rights and privileges unite, and thus the beginning of a new family group is formed.

To determine definitely even the important
organic features of the family system is, according
to Hewitt, as yet impossible in the case of the
Indian tribes north of the border. Swanton, in
referring to the tribes of the north-west coast,
says that in addition to the husband, wife and
children, a household was often increased by a
number of relatives who lived with the house-
owner on almost equal terms. Again, in tribes
where gentile or clan organisation did not exist,
incest groups on both paternal and maternal
sides are largely determined by a system of
relationships fixing the status and position of
every person within an indefinite group, which
is to say that marriage and cohabitation may
not subsist between persons related to each
other except within definitely prescribed limits
on both sides, though kinship may be recognised
as extending beyond this area.

The common Iroquoian name for the maternal
blood family was *ohwachira* and was known to
all dialects of this stock. On the contrary there
are found among these various dialects names
designating the group known as the clan which
would indicate the probability that the family

as such antedated the development of clan organisation.

The intimate relations of family life and the laws governing family customs are wholly administered within that circle, and such laws constitute the daily rules of action. When the family as a unit becomes absorbed in a higher form of society, certain individual rights are acquired, as for instance that of appealing to the higher tribunal. Wealth and power of the family or clan depended usually on the number of its members.

The condition of women among the Indians of America has long been misunderstood and, when considered at all, frequently placed in an erroneous light, the female being usually regarded as a slave and drudge both before and after her marriage. This misconceived view, due largely to inaccurate observation, may possibly have been correct in some isolated cases and particularly among certain tribes possessing but few of the elements of social organisation, especially those which were non-agricultural.

The status of woman depended to a great extent upon conditions having their origin in habitat, climate and various concepts arising often from mythology as well as economic environment. For example; broad distinctions were made between women belonging to or not belonging to a certain tribe or community. As a rule the woman was looked upon by the men of the tribe as their equal. Matters pertaining to the home fell to the sphere of the woman. In addition to the numerous activities which they shared in common with the men, there was also the care of the children. It was the lot of the female to attend to the tanning of skins, the weaving of materials for clothing and other uses, the making of mats and baskets, to become potters and workers in wood, to sew, dye, gather and store roots, seeds, berries, plants, and to dry and smoke the meat procured by the men.

The care of the camping utensils and all family belongings also fell to her, though in this she was assisted by children of sufficient age or the in-capacitated men of the tribe, indeed the essential governing the division of labour and responsi-bility between the sexes lies deeper than what, for want of a better name, was generally supposed to have been the tyranny of man. At the time of planting it was thought that the sowing of seed by women rendered such seed more fertile, therefore sowing and cultivating came strictly within her domain.

Many of the early travellers have commented on the condition of a woman's life among the tribes, though it would appear that, strenuous as the toil may have been, it evidently affected her but slightly. There is little doubt that the records of the first explorers are somewhat exaggerated if not biassed, inasmuch as their minds were prejudiced as they observed customs so vastly different from those with which they were previously acquainted. Equal in number have been those who have taken opposite views.

Among the Iroquois and similarly organised tribes many fundamental institutions of society were controlled by woman: as an instance—descent of blood or citizenship in the clan, hence in the tribe, was traced through her; titles, distinguished by unchanging specific names, of the various chieftainships of the tribe belonged exclusively to her; the lodge and all its furnishings and equipment were hers; her offspring belonged to her; the lands of the clan, and so of the tribe, as the source of food, life and shelter belonged to her, and in consequence of these possessions and these vested rights, hers was the sovereign right to select from among her sons candidates for the chieftainship of her own clan,

and so, eventually, of the tribe. As the source of
the life of the clan, the sole right to adopt aliens
was vested in the woman; mothers possessed
authority to forbid sons going on the warpath,
and, lastly, woman had the power of life and
death over such alien prisoners as became her
share in the spoils of war.

There were chieftainesses among various
eastern tribes who were of first importance, some
of whom on certain occasions succeeded the male
incumbent of such an office, and it is evident
from the above that the authority possessed by
the Indian husband over his wife or wives was far
from absolute, early observers to the contrary notwithstanding. The wife enjoyed in large measure
an independence, and as a rule her influence over
her husband was marked. Her status varied, as
has been mentioned, according to location and
also according to the institutions preserved by the
tribe in question. In some instances she was the
equal, in others she was the superior of the man.

In nearly all tribes possessing rudiments of
social organisation, woman was sole master of
her own body. Violation of their own or alien
women was rare and regarded with horror
and aversion. According to Westermarck, the
Navaho husband possessed but little authority

over his wife, even though obtained by payment
of the bride price or present. It would appear,
therefore, in summing up, that woman enjoyed
a large if not preponderating amount of independence reckoned largely in proportion to the extent
of the community's dependence for substance on
the product of her activity.

It is almost impossible to give a comprehensive description of marriage among the
American aborigines. Such unions depended
largely on economic considerations varying to
a wonderful degree as between the Eskimo of
the north and the Pueblos of the south-west.
Ceremony of any kind is barred with the former
and little if any exists among the latter, though
representing a much higher stage of culture and
having a developed clan organisation. The Zuni
bridegroom is adopted as a son by the father of
the betrothed and married life begins at her home.
Among the Atlantic tribes of Algonquian stock
the rule against marriage within the clan or gens
was strictly enforced.

Polygamy seems to have been more generally practised among the Plains Indians than
elsewhere, the younger sisters of a first wife
being potential wives of the husband. An almost universal custom throughout the continent

governs the matter of separation. Wives can leave cruel husbands and the husband may discard an unruly or otherwise disagreeable spouse. Divorce is generally discreditable but easily effected, children going with the mother. Monogamy is, however, the prevalent form of marriage among the majority of Indian families. Though the economic factor is everywhere potent, actual purchase is uncommon. The marriage tie is on the whole loose and with few exceptions can be dissolved by the wife as well as the husband.

Under this system which allows such easy dissolution of the family bond the most important factor in domestic life is the child. The relation of the Indian parents to their children brings forth the highest traits of aboriginal character. Both parents are, with rare exceptions, devoted to their offspring, upon whom they bestow the fullest expression of affection and solicitude. Among the Plains Indians the arrival of a new baby is the cause of considerable comment. The father's first act is to prepare the wooden frame of the cradle which becomes the portable bed until the child is able to walk. This in turn is decorated by the grandmother or some woman expert in

bead or quill work. The newly born infant is
treated to a cold bath and given in charge of some
matron until the mother's health is restored, and
in some tribes, notably the Hopi, ashes or sacred
meal is rubbed on the child at birth.

Lactation continues for long periods, often two
years. With all her affection the mother is seldom
conversant with even the first principles of sani-
tation, feeding and care, and consequently infant
mortality is great in nearly all tribes, a very
small proportion coming to maturity.

Opposed to the general supposition is the
fact that children are not continually kept in
the cradle, but only during a journey or while
being carried from place to place. While at
home the child rolls about on the grass or on
a bed, without restraint. Little or no clothing
is worn except in extreme weather, this being
especially true of the period between the ages of
five and ten years and this practice still prevails
among some tribes.

The child may or may not be named at birth,
and in any event the privilege of assuming one
of more importance or significance can be used if
desired. The right of naming is often relegated to
the grandparent. Twins are frequently regarded
as uncanny, and feared in some instances as

possessors of occult powers. Boring the ears
for pendants is often the occasion of more or less
ceremony, particularly among the Plains tribes,
and the first tattooing and first insertion of the
labret[1] are memorable events.

At from fourteen to sixteen years of age the
boy, particularly among the Atlantic tribes, made
solitary fast and vigil for the purpose of obtaining
communication with the medicine spirit which
was to be his protector through life, after which,
by passing through certain ordeals, the youth
became competent to take his place as a man
among warriors. At about this period, or possibly
a year or two earlier, his sister's friends may have
gathered to celebrate her puberty dance, and the
child life for both has thus ended.

A description of the religious tenets of the
Indian must be brief. Their concepts divide
themselves into two groups and in that way they
must be referred to—those concerning the individual and those touching the clan, gens or
tribe. As a basis of religious life stands the belief
in the existence of a supernatural or magic power.
This may influence man and in turn be acted
upon by him, and this conception of a Deity is
almost universal. It is variously designated

[1] See note p. 152.

Manito, as among the Algonquian, Wakonda by the Sioux, Oreda by the Iroquois, etc., and, notwithstanding a slight difference in signification, the basic thought of all is that a power inherent in the objects of nature is more potent than the natural power of man.

The occult or theosophic connexion between the Indian's religious concepts and his mythology is marked and will not be dwelt upon here, as it is covered more fully from the latter standpoint in a succeeding chapter.

One of the chief aims in the religious experience of the Indian is to gain control over, or acquire for himself, some one of the supernatural powers and thereby make it subservient to his own will and needs. This process, usually called the procuring of the manito, is attempted generally by the young men during the period of adolescence, and includes fasting, bathing, vomiting and other means of thoroughly cleansing the body so that it may be perfectly acceptable to a Higher Being.

At the same time the youth, by means of drugs, dancing or similar actions causing temperamental excitement, works himself into a trance during which a vision of his guardian spirit appears, thereafter acting as a protector

through life. He obtains special abilities through
the acquisition of this power and by invoking its
aid may become a superior warrior, a shaman,
or a successful hunter, or he may amass riches.
Victory in games, or ability to acquire the love
of women may also follow.

Another means of obtaining this religious
power may be through inheritance or by specific
prayer. By the latter method certain accredited
formulae (or prayer sticks as among the Pueblos)
are used, which are meant to convey a man's
wishes to the Powers. Sacrifices and human
offerings were not, on the whole, used so extensively in North America as in other parts of
the world, though instances of self-torture, particularly among the Mandans and other Siouan
tribes, must be reckoned with.

Included among the many popular though
fallacious beliefs regarding the Indian was that
concerning his most mighty deity "the Great
Spirit." As has been shown above, his religious
ideas were manifold, and his chief object was to
propitiate by supplication or self-sacrifice each
and every one. To no special deity was ascribed
moral good or evil, yet these spirits were the
source of all good or bad fortune whether on the
warpath or hunting trail, or at work or play.

Success led him to adore, offer sacrifices and make presents of value; defeated he cast his manito from him and made offering forthwith to a more powerful or more friendly deity. In this spiritualistic world he dwelt in continual fear. To offend the spirit of the dark wood, the lake or the prairie was his constant dread, and his daily prayer was for assistance against disease in one form or another.

On the whole the American natives incline strongly toward all forms of religious excitement. This is demonstrated not only by the high development of ancient religious forms but also by the frequency with which prophets have appeared among them.

Between this body of spirits and materialistic man came as mediators the shamans and priests. The authority of the former depended wholly on individual action, whereas the latter represented to a certain extent some form of society.

According to Swanton, the most highly developed priesthood, north of Mexico, is found among the Pueblos of the south-west. Here it controls the civil and military branches of the tribe. On the other hand, among various tribes of the east, the order divides and subdivides, as with the Chippewa there were found the wâbĕnō', those who practised medicine and magic, the jĕs'-sakkī'd, known as seers and prophets, and the midĕ', members of the sacred society. The shamans were also of two or more classes according to locality.

The matter of disease and its cure among the Indians, while important, can be merely touched upon. Illness was to a great extent a mystery and treated as such, coming therefore to a certain degree under the care of the spiritual adviser as well as the medicine-man. Formerly every tribe had a number of such thaumaturgi often including both male and female, who were considered possessed of supernatural powers enabling them to recognise and eventually cure disease. Their popularity or influence over the people depended largely on actual ability, and there were specialists along certain lines as among the more advanced races. Surgery in a primitive form was practised by the more accomplished; trephining was known, but not north of Mexico.

Another class of medicine men and women corresponded closely to our own herbalists and to the midwives among the rural white people. Women predominated, though they formed no societies nor were they so highly respected as the other class.

Before the advent of the civilised races on the North American continent it is presumed that the Indian was, on the whole, a comparatively healthy people. No evidence has been found from which to gather data as to the prevailing diseases, though illness in some form was of course prevalent but probably not in serious or epidemic form. Doubt is even expressed as to whether small-pox, tuberculosis, pre-Columbian syphilis, typhus, cancer, scarlet fever, cholera or rachitis were known. In any event they were rare.

Though containing much of the robust constitution the Indians are in general at the present time subject to many disorders common to the white race. This, however, is more true of the mixed bloods than the pure. There is little suffering from idiocy, or insanity, and cretinism is exceedingly rare, paresis being quite unknown. Venereal diseases, not uncommon among the degraded, are carefully guarded and usually avoided by the better informed[1].

In a list of the destroyers of the aborigines all but two, war and, possibly, tuberculosis, may be said to have come from the white man. Small-pox and other epidemics, sexual diseases,

[1] See note p. 152.

whiskey and attendant dissipation, starvation and unaccustomed conditions, a low vitality, have caused a decrease in a once numerous race.

The somewhat appalling state of Indian mortality was set forth in a message from ex-President Taft during August of 1912, a portion of which is here quoted: "Last year (1911) of over 42,000 Indians examined for disease, over 16 per cent. of them had trachoma...so easily spread that it threatens both the Indian communities and their white neighbours....Of the 40,000 Indians examined, 6800 had tuberculosis. The death rate in the Indian country is 35 per thousand, as compared with 15 per thousand—the average death rate for the United States as a whole. No exact figures are yet available for infant mortality among Indians, but field studies now being made show that while proportionately more Indian babies than white babies are born, very many more Indian babies die. Few Indian homes anywhere have proper sanitary conditions, and in many instances the bad condition of their domestic surroundings is almost beyond belief."

The dying off of the race leads Mooney to conclude after a careful study of this phase of the subject that there has been a reduction in the population, from that originally found by the white men, of 65 per cent. For that territory north of the Mexican border a total of 1,500,000 Indians has been estimated as living during the fifteenth century. This first number is now reduced to about 403,000, including the Indians of British America, Alaska and Greenland.

CHAPTER IV

THE PLAINS INDIANS

In this and the following chapter brief historical sketches are given covering two general divisions of the Indian families of America, namely those in the central or prairie regions who are known as the Plains Indians, and those of the south-western portion of the United States, ethnologically classified as the Indians of the South-west. These comprise stocks which are to a certain extent separate and distinct.

As will be observed by a glance at the linguistic map the singularly unequal geographic distribution of the various stocks in no way tends to assist the student of ethnology. A most remarkable gathering of dialects, in fact more than four-fifths of the total number, is to be found among the peoples distributed along the Pacific coast from Alaska to the peninsula of Lower California. Opposing this view some of the great families such as the Athapascan, Algonquian, Shoshonean, Siouan and Iroquoian extend over vast areas which include both mountain and plain and woodland, while the Eskimauan family borders the whole Arctic coastal section from Alaska to the Island of Newfoundland in the extreme north-east.

The Plains Indians, occupying that immense area eastward from the slopes of the Pacific ranges, are to be looked upon as in many respects the representatives of their race, though in reality their territory includes, if the stock or family be considered, practically the whole country from the mountains to the Atlantic seaboard.

For the purpose of further subdividing the subject in this chapter, three tribes are to be considered as typical, selected from a like number of families as follows : the Cheyenne, Algonquian; the Iowa, Siouan; the Pawnee, Caddoan. Each is of prime importance and illustrates, in the first and second named, at least two of the largest and most prominent stocks, and comprises, with the single exception of the Iroquoian, the most important of all north of the Mexican border.

Inasmuch as climatic conditions and environment have brought about a mode of life in many respects different from that on the Pacific slope and in the extreme south, the change in cultural habits is therefore equally noticeable. Furthermore it must be said that the Indians, particularly those among whom certain arts or crafts had in any way advanced, were never negative in character. Their place in the history of America is as clear as that of any of the peoples who encroached from without. They were writing in rude characters before England had received her Magna Charta, and understood musical notes in a degree before the Psalms were chanted at Rome. The sun, moon and stars were worshipped while Egypt was yet pondering over the phenomenon of the Milky Way, and their literature, legend or myth, is as old as the Nibelungen Lied.

These facts, to be sure, must be held within limit. There were classes and grades among the aborigines, and what is cited above must apply for the great part to the more advanced even among those noted. The Indians with whom the Europeans first came in contact were superior in many respects to their brethren both west and south, and, as has already been shown, the ethical status had been cultivated to a high degree among many of the tribes of the north-west.

The Cheyenne tribe of the great Algonquian family is of peculiar interest to the ethnologist as an example of non-roving agricultural people developed by unusual circumstances, within a comparatively recent period, into a body of nomads.

They have passed through such a complete change
of habit and ceremony that their former life is
recalled now only in sacred tradition, though
fully proven by documentary evidence and un-
mistakable fact. All that they have to-day of
tribal life, with the exception of the Medicine
Arrow rite, has been obtained during their course
of migration and their oldest ceremonies date
back no farther than two centuries.

This tribe is widely known and under various
appellations. The popular idea that their name
is derived from the French *chien*, dog, is wholly
erroneous. It was in fact given to them by
the Sioux, viz.: Shahi-yena, Shai-ena or Shai-
ela, which interpreted means, according to the
missionaries Williamson and Riggs, "people of
alien speech," the name likewise being used by
the Sioux for the Cree Indians of Canada. As in
the case of many other important tribes they had
their distinctive sign, for the purpose of that form
of language—a gesture which means "cut arms"
or "cut fingers," made by drawing the right index
finger across the left several times in rapid
succession. This has also variously been interpreted as "striped arrows," and they were
so designated by the Caddo, Comanche, Hidatsa
and Shoshoni.

As near as can be definitely ascertained, the
earliest authentic location of the Cheyenne,
previous to 1700, seems to have been in what is
now south-eastern Minnesota, and according to
their own national tradition, still current in the
tribe, they arrived at this point after wandering
extensively through a cold and desolate country
in the north, probably to be taken as Canada. A
first positive mention of them, under the name
of Chaa, is made by La Salle at the time of a visit
made by a party of the tribe to his Fort Crève-
cœur, on the Illinois river. They came, as they
explained, from the head of "the great river"
(Mississippi) with the request that the French
should come to their country for furs.

According to an apparently trustworthy tradition which is still current among them, the
Cheyenne preceded the Sioux in their occupation
of the Mississippi river region and were found by
the latter on their arrival. The Iowa at this time
also occupied lower Minnesota directly to the
south, and the Oto to the west. These facts are
mentioned as corroborative evidence of the early
habitat of the Cheyenne who, at a later period,
moved to what is known as the Cheyenne branch
of the Red river in North Dakota, the name
for that stream being thus acquired but known

also to the Sioux as "the place where the Shai-ena planted." From this proof it is deduced that the tribe was still an agricultural people.

The first causes toward an upheaval and migration were essentially two in number. With the establishment of the English trading posts on Hudson Bay in 1668, the Cree, also of Algonquian stock and the largest tribe, then as now, in Canada, formed close alliance with the traders and began a policy of pressure and general ousting of neighbouring bands. This internecine warfare was encouraged by both French and English, particularly by the former, who were advancing westward along the lakes and northwards toward the upper waters of the Mississippi. In consequence of this pressure it is known that the Sioux and other tribes in the vicinity were gradually pushed onward toward the Missouri before the close of the eighteenth century. In this involuntary migration the Cheyenne undoubtedly led, being, as it would seem, most remote from other nations and least adept in the manner of coping with the more advanced methods of warfare.

Hence a second cause. Those tribes bordering more on the edges of civilisation came sooner to know the value of fire-arms and to adopt them for their own use. This unquestionably hastened the movement of the Cheyenne, who had no fire-arms.

As late as 1700, when Le Sueur built his trading post on the lower Minnesota, he was told that the river belonged to the Iowa, Oto and Teton (Sioux), and inasmuch as no mention is made of the Cheyenne it would seem probable that they had already moved since the period of La Salle, twenty years before. Whether the actual migration of this tribe to the region of the great Plains was due wholly to the efforts of the Cree in the beginning, is a difficult question, but the fact of their later movement from the Red river country to the Missouri and thence to the region of the Black Hills was brought about entirely by Siouan hostility.

They were met by the explorers Lewis and Clark, first in 1804 and again two years later, and in their report these travellers make the positive statement that the tribe at one time lived on the Cheyenne branch of the Red river, where they had cultivated corn before they were driven west by the Sioux. Thus from an agricultural people they became roving buffalo hunters, nomadic in the strict sense.

With the first years of the eighteenth century the fur traders had come among them but little. They arranged among themselves to transfer the robes to the Hudson Bay Company stations by way of the Arikara villages on the Missouri, and they continued in a defensive war with the Sioux, and up to a certain period, with the Mandan. Later travellers as Bradbury in 1817 and Porter in 1829 corroborate earlier statements as to the western migration, and from the last date until 1870 various writers acquainted with the tribe continue the history. The point that is made, however, is that from a sedentary they became a wandering people; that they once lived in permanent villages subsisting on their own corn, fish and wild ducks, though it is important to notice that no mention is made of rice. At an early date they made pottery, an art now lost, and the skin tipi, or tent, was in use. This last has of course been abandoned.

As referred to above, the early history of the tribe is lost in tradition. Legends among them tell of a people living to the north-west of their early home, known as the Moiseo, who accompanied them in their first moves but later turned back "hungering for the ducks of the lakes." It is believed these companions may have been the Monsoni, an Algonquian tribe of British America, often classed as part of the Cree, though there is no separate enumeration of them in official Canadian reports. To the west or south-west were the Sutaio, at first their enemies but later incorporated and to-day existing only as a division of the Cheyenne. Living farther to the west these last seem to have been a buffalo tribe as distinguished from their neighbours. To them also belonged what was known as the "Buffalo-Cap Medicine" which with its sacred ritual and tradition is still preserved and regarded as second only to the Sacred Arrows.

One other traditional tribe met the Cheyenne after crossing the Missouri, and this was known, according to Mooney, as the Ŏ wŭ′qeo. Being hostile, they were surprised by a superior force of their foe and driven on to the ice-bound river where, being unable to stand or flee, they were massacred with the exception of one woman whom the Cheyenne chief took to wife. Learning the language of her captors she informed him concerning the government of the Ŏ wŭ′qeo and so impressed those who heard the narration that under her instructions they set up a chief tipi, and trimmed and painted a bundle of "chief-sticks" on the plan which still continues among this tribe.   This was, according to the records of early travellers, the beginning of their present council system.

As in the instance of the Sauk and Fox, the Cheyenne have for a long period been closely associated with the Arapaho so that the compound tribal designation has become most familiar.   The languages are both Algonquian though not mutually intelligible.   In habit, dress and much of the ceremony the tribes are closely identified, but tradition is mute as to when the association was first formed.

Many of those who first penetrated into the interior of America have made mention of the Cheyenne though the references are not always clear.   Carver, for example, writes of the Shians in 1768 but confuses them with the Sioux.   In 1802 Alexander Henry, the younger, mentions the tribe as having been driven from the Red river country in Canada, and in the same year the Frenchman Perrin du Lac met a party of Cheyenne at the White river who had never before seen Europeans.   Lewis and Clark (*loc. cit.*) met them two years later for the first time, and in 1811, W. P. Hunt, en route from St Louis to Astoria, sojourned among them two weeks for the purpose of buying horses.

This tribe, together with the two others that follow, are selected as typical Plains Indians. The first, in common with the others, has passed through the vicissitudes of life common to the aborigines. Gradually they have relinquished their freehold rights, if it can be considered that such existed, and year after year with the advance of the white man they have retreated farther west. Their first treaty with the United States was in 1825 and others followed in due course. Gradually they were pressed from one point to another until now the tribe is on reservations in Montana, South Dakota and Oklahoma with a total population of about 3000 souls.

Their social organisation is interesting and in many details typical of the Plains tribes. This was based on the camp circle under which system they were divided into ten principal sections, each of which occupied a definite position in the circle, and this arrangement was made especially clear when they assembled for the celebration of some important function, as, for example, the Sun Dance. This camp circle, like the single tipi, opened toward the east, while the order of progression followed the sun, that is to say from the entrance at the east, around to south and west, hence north and to the place of beginning.

The important divisions were each named and there were in addition so-called warrior societies, composed usually of from eight to twelve members. Six such societies, according to Dorsey, are, among the Cheyenne, known collectively as nŭ'tqio, i.e. "warriors," and each is clearly designated. Some are of higher standing than others, though each is distinct.

During late years the native society organisation of the Cheyenne has been greatly demoralised by the introduction of what is termed the Omaha Dance Society, originating as the name implies, among the latter tribe. Spectacular and free from many burdensome features this new dance has won favour among many of the Plains tribes, but has lost much of its early interest.

Guilds, or at least what might be termed closer organisations than those called societies, are numerous. These somewhat select groupings are known among the Indians themselves as medicine societies. They are formed especially to guard the tribal secrets pertaining to healing or magic and are under several heads, or what may be defined as departments, many of which are now obsolete. The most noted of these were known as the Fire Dance and Crazy Dance, the first having a membership of ten or a dozen persons. These fanatics possessed or claimed to possess a vegetable ointment which was applied to the naked feet, after which the members danced over beds of living coals until they had reduced the mass to cinders. At other times they would chew burning coals or plunge their arms into boiling water without seeming effect. According to the missionary Riggs, who was for some time among the Cheyenne, this last act was carried on after having previously deadened the skin by applications of sheep sorrel (*rumex acetosella*).

The Crazy Dancers, for their part, claimed knowledge of a certain secret plant, after chewing which, they became temporarily insane, and possessed of superhuman strength. While under its influence they were able to throw men about like children, jump extraordinary distances, carry weights far beyond those ordinarily within their ability, and performed many other abnormal acts.

Even among the women societies prevailed for dancing, healing and other purposes. These, however, were not numerous, though until recently a sort of woman's union had absolute control of the decorative arts and crafts of the tribe.

A peculiar rite or system still holds among the

younger men of the tribe known in translation as
"taking a friend." In this system, which is a
form of comradeship, two young men, generally
members of the same warrior society, practically
adopt each other as brothers, being so recognised
thereafter by their own family and relatives as well
as by their friends at large. They hold property
in common, live with one another, and this act
of mutual fellowship often continues through life,
marriage on either side not affecting it, and the
true relationship is exemplified frequently in
most unusual examples of daring, rescues or
self-denial.

As compared with other Plains tribes the
shield of the Cheyenne is crude. Every man
upon becoming a full-fledged warrior is expected
to possess such an article for use in battle as
well as for decorative or heraldic purpose,
displaying in full the owner's special, family or
military designation. This shield is sacred and
guarded by means of religious taboo. So, too,
formerly was the tipi heraldry applied to
decorative designs and regulations hereditary
in certain families. Neither shield nor heraldry
system is as elaborate among them as among
certain other tribes of this locality, notably the
Kiowa, yet Mooney has shown it to be more

recent among the last named who, however, preceded the Cheyenne both in occupancy of the
Plains region and in the acquisition of the horse.

The religious life of this particular branch of
the Algonquian family is less important than
might be supposed, and may be said to centre
almost wholly about the great ceremonies of the
Sacred Arrows and the Sun Dance. Possessing
from the very beginning the four sacred arrows
with the accompanying ritual and tradition they
naturally hold them in the highest veneration,
few of the priests or older men even daring
to mention them freely or even by name,
the whole past and future of the tribe being
identified with them and their great culture hero,
Motsioyóïf. Under no circumstances are women
allowed to look upon or even approach the
sacred bundle. Only on certain occasions, as
for example the wiping of the stain of blood
from the people when a Cheyenne has been slain
by a tribesman, are the arrows exposed to public
view of the men. In the former days of war and
conquest these arrows were carried on the battle-
field, and indeed by this method two of the
originals were lost to the Pawnee, though later
replaced in duplicate, and they now rest with
the tradition-keeper and custodian of the sacred

bundle, near Cantonment, Oklahoma, a place which is also the present headquarters of the most conservative element of the tribe. One of the last ceremonies of the Sacred Arrows was performed in 1904.

The Sun Dance is not uncommon in some form among nearly all the larger Plains tribes, and was given to the Cheyenne by the Sutaio at the time when peace was first made between them. It is a part of the tradition of this latter band and sacred. This fact explains to some extent the origin of the Buffalo-Cap Medicine from Domsïvï'sts, the supernatural culture hero. This Medicine as well as tradition still exists in the keeping of the priest of this ritual. The ceremony of the Sun Dance is, as far as possible, kept from the knowledge of the white man.

A sketch of the home life would be but a narrative of that which is common to all the Indians of the Plains, who dwelt originally in skin tipis and hunted the buffalo. Their mortuary customs were of the usual sort, the dead being generally laid away on scaffolds or in branches of trees. They were occasionally placed in boxes upon the surface of the earth, and quite frequently in graves, but they were never cremated.

The Cheyenne are generally good types of

manhood in both build and stature, and according to the best authority rank somewhat above the average in courage. As examples of the native American the tribe may be studied with profit, yet even among these Indians the very blood has changed because of intermarriage and incorporation of captives as well as other causes. On the other hand their culture is not in any degree ancient. There is a newness about everything that they have with the exception of the Sacred Arrows cult, and they may be said to have completely lost their old life and adopted so much from other tribes of the Plains that, were it not for their Algonquian affinity and the positive facts known concerning their history, it would be difficult to recognise in these rovers the people of earth lodges and planters of corn near the head waters of the Mississippi. Even their great cultural rites of to-day are new. Their scalp cult is possibly modern, they borrowed the Sun Dance from one tribe and their council system from another, so also the Omaha and Ghost Dances, and their warrior organisation, to mention but one form, is of recent development. The customs among them that exist at present differ from those of even ten years since.

The second tribe to be described and one of

no less importance as distinctive of the Great
Prairie Region, is the Iowa of the great Siouan
family. These Indians have been included by
Dorsey, both ethnographically and linguistically,
with the Oto and Missouri tribes, thus forming
the so-called "Chiwere" group; a term when
literally translated meaning "belonging to this
place," or "the home people." The real difference existing between the tribes here noted is
one of dialect only. Traditional evidence proves
conclusively that they sprung originally from
that stem which appears to have been the parent
stock of certain other south-western Siouan
tribes, namely the Winnebago, and from direct
information obtained from their people as late
as 1883, investigators have ascertained that not
only the Iowa, Missouri and Oto tribes were
from the same source but that the Ponca and
Omaha could without question be included as
having once formed part of the Winnebago
nation.

From their primal home to the north of the
Great Lakes, as tradition has it, came the fore-
bears of this tribe. Attracted by the abundance
of fish, the Winnebago halted on the shores
of Lake Michigan, while the other bands continued south-westward, eventually coming to the

Mississippi. At this point another division took place and it was here that the Iowa separated from the larger group. It was also at this period that they received the name of Pahoja or Grey Snow. Without stopping for any length of time, after leaving their comrades they continued down the general course of the Mississippi until Rock river (in Illinois) was reached. Here as on other occasions in the early history of the tribe, much must depend on hearsay. Certain traditions, however, place them farther north, and a map drawn in 1848 by Waw-non-que-skoon-a, an Iowa Indian, shows their movements quite clearly until that date.

There is a tradition still popular among the Sioux that, when their ancestors first came to the Falls of St Anthony, the Iowa tribe occupied the country adjacent to the Minnesota river and that the Cheyenne occupied territory farther up the same stream.

On the arrival of Le Sueur in 1701 for the purpose of erecting his fort near the mouth of the Blue Earth river, many of the tribe were found and messengers were sent to invite them to settle in the vicinity of the stockade, because of their excellence in farming and general husbandry. Those dispatched for this purpose

found that the Indians had recently moved westward toward the Missouri, as they wished to be
closer to the Omaha who then dwelt in that
region. The tribes with whom Le Sueur came
in contact informed him that the river upon
which he was about to settle belonged to the
Sioux of the West (Dakota), the Ayavois (Iowa),
and the Otoctatas (Oto), who lived near by.
Probably the first white man to come in actual
contact with the Iowa was Père André, who
referred to them in 1676, at which time they
were situated about two hundred miles west of
Green Bay, Wisconsin.

The next reference made by a European seems
to be that of Father Zenobius Membré in 1680,
who mentions the Authontontas (Oto) and the
Nadouessious Maskoutens (Iowa) "about 130
leagues from the Illinois river in three great
villages built near a river which empties into the
Colbert (Mississippi) on the west side above the
Illinois, almost opposite the mouth of the Wisconsin." He also seems to locate a portion of
the Aiuoves (probably Aioues) to the west of the
Milwaukee river.

On Marquette's manuscript map which accompanied his *Journal*, 1673, the Pahoutet (Iowa)
are placed on or near the Missouri river in close

company with the Maha (Omaha) and the Onton-
tana (Oto). This is no doubt conjecture on the
part of the cartographer. The Sieur de la Salle
knew of both Oto and Iowa, and among his letters
is one referring to Father Hennepin, dated
August 22, 1682, in which he mentions them as
Otoutanta and Atounauea respectively. He
further states that one of his company was
familiar with the languages of both these tribes
which, however, is doubtful.

When Le Sueur first supplied these Indians
with fire-arms in 1700 they were located at the
extreme headquarters of the Des Moines river,
though from the translation of this explorer's
narrative, as contained in the Collections of the
Wisconsin Historical Society, it would seem that
this band and the Oto removed and "established
themselves toward the Missouri river, near the
Maha." In Jefferys' *French Dominions in North
and South America*, 1760, the Iowa are located on
the Mississippi in latitude 43° 30'. Singularly
enough his map places them on the east side of
the Missouri, west of the sources of the Des
Moines river and above the Oto, who were on
the west side of the Missouri and below the
Omaha. According to Lewis and Clark, as given
in Coues' edition of 1893, the villages of the

Iowa consisted "of 300 men...on the river Des Moines." The map by Waw-non-que-skoon-a, as included in Schoolcraft's great work, gives the final stopping place of the tribe at a point near the junction of the Wolf and Missouri rivers, within the limits of the present State of Nebraska. Some authorities give their ultimate location as being in two villages, one on the Platte and another on the Great Nemaha river, from which places they conducted traffic with the traders from St Louis, dealing principally in beaver, otter, racoon, deer and bear skins.

They also appear to have been cultivators of the soil to some extent, even at this early date, and it is recorded that Le Sueur made efforts to have them locate near his Fort l'Huillier as they were "industrious and accustomed to cultivate the earth." In addition to corn they grew beans, and the explorer Pike says "they cultivated corn but not proportionately as much as did the Sauks and Foxes." This writer also states that they were less civilised than the latter.

At a much earlier date Père André writes that, while their village was a large one they were poor as a tribe, their greatest wealth being in ox-hides and "red calumets," indicating thereby that the Iowa early traded in the manufactured

catlinite[1] pipes. In many customs that prevailed
among the Iowa it has been found that they
differed but little from cognate tribes. In their
visiting and marriage relations they were not unlike the Omaha and others closely allied among
the Dakota. The camp circle was divided into
half-circles and occupied by two phratries of four
gentes each. The first phratry regulated the hunt
and other affairs pertaining to the tribe during the
autumn and winter. Throughout the other parts
of the year the lead was taken by the other phratry.
In a general way, however, the Iowa social institution differs but slightly from others of the Siouan
stock. Children are managed similarly to those
of neighbouring tribes. Formerly murder was
punished with death by the nearest of kin or by
some friend of the murdered person. Occasionally presents were made to the avengers of the
murder, in consequence of which the crime was
condoned.

Like many other Mississippi Valley tribes the
Iowa are not to any great extent associated with
the tumuli of America. With the exception of
some few mounds in Wapello county, Iowa, at a
point near Iowaville, the site of an early trading
post, there is little evidence that the Iowa were

[1] See note p. 152.

in any way connected with the mounds of the State. Along the valley located in this section were many spots frequented by both the Sauk and Fox as well as Iowa, and here also were situated the famous race tracks of nearly a mile in length, belonging to the latter tribe.

The various games indulged in by these Indians differed but slightly from those in vogue among kindred or allied tribes. As is almost universal, dice games, or games of chance are more generally popular, while the games of dexterity take second place. Catlin describes, under the former class, one called Kon-tho-gra, or the game of the platter, which is played almost exclusively by women. It is said to be exceedingly fascinating and consists of little blocks of wood marked with certain points and colours for counting. These are then shaken in a bowl and thrown out on a sort of pillow. The counters thus thoroughly mixed, bets are made while the bowl still covers the dice. The one among the contestants who has chosen the fortunate numbers and colours shown when the bowl is removed wins. Another game described by Catlin is called Ing-Kee-Ko-Kee, or the game of the moccasin. It was played to a song accompaniment among the Iowa by two, by four or by six people seated on the ground in

a circle. In the centre were placed three or four
moccasins under one of which the players in turn
tried to conceal some small article such as a nut
or a stone. The opponents chose what appeared
to be the lucky covering and if successful took the
stakes. The game, according to this writer, appeared simple and almost foolish, yet he professes
to have seen it played for hours without inter-
mission and in perfect musical rhythm, and states
that it "forms one of the principal gambling
games of these gambling people."

Among the Omaha, Ponca, Oto and Iowa the
game of Arrow ($Ma^{n'}muqpe$) was most common.
This however was more of a religious game, and
is now practically obsolete since the introduction
of fire-arms. Arrows were shot up into trees
until they lodged in the branches. The players
then tried to dislodge them and whoever brought
down the first, won. There were no sides or
opposing parties.

Probably the most exciting and in many
respects the most important game among the
tribes of the Plains is that of Ball-playing or
Racket. This is distinctly a man's game as
opposed to double-ball and some other forms
commonly played by women, though it may be
remarked the Racket is occasionally played

among the Santee Sioux by both sexes together. This game has been divided into two principal classes, that of the single and that of the double racket or bat; the latter is more especially peculiar to the southern tribes. The racket may be likewise termed a throwing stick as it is used to pick up and throw the ball rather than for the purpose of hitting. The ball is either of wood or of buckskin stuffed with hair, and the usual size is about two and one-half inches in diameter. Various kinds of rackets are used by the players, some preferring long and some short handles. Among the Oto of Oklahoma, one measured was forty inches in length.

Catlin gives an excellent description of this game among the Iowa. His details concerning the goals and byes and various points connected with the different features of the game make his sketch one of the most complete available.

As among all tribes east and west, north and south, the Iowa were devoted to their numerous dances, many of which were of the highest importance. Mention is made here only of several of the more common or necessary ones, as the subject is one which, if treated fully, would occupy a volume in itself.

The peculiar dance known as the Welcome

Dance is given in honour of one or more strangers whom the tribe may decide to welcome to their village. The musicians as well as spectators, out of due respect, all rise to their feet while it is being performed. The song which accompanies it is at first one of lament but ends in a gay and lively manner.

The War Dance is usually the most exciting as well as the longest and most tiresome of all the dances. As a rule it is divided into three parts as follows : (*a*) the Warriors' Dance—Eh-Ros-Ka —given generally after a party had returned from war both as a boast as well as an amusement. The song used at this time entitled War Song, or Wa-Sissica, appeared to be addressed to the body of an enemy, from the name Eh-Ros-Ka, meaning tribe, war party or body.

The most spirited part of this greatest of all dances was called (*b*) the Approaching Dance, in which the dancers by their gestures exhibited the methods of advancing on an enemy. The song in this portion is also similar to that above mentioned.

Ha-Kon-E-Crase, or the Eagle Dance, (*c*) more familiarly known as "the soaring eagle," forms the third and most pleasing part of the War Dance and is in every respect an extremely interesting spectacle. Each dancer imagines himself a bird on the wing, and as they dance forward from behind the musicians they take the position of an eagle headed against the wind and about to swoop down on some unsuspecting prey. They have a strange method of singing and whistling at the same time.

The Calumet Dance, the Ball-play Dance, the Scalp Dance, the Buffalo Dance and the Bear Dance are all important but vary very slightly from those executed for similar purposes among other tribes of the same family. What has been said about the dances applies with equal force to the songs and music. The War Song, Death Song, Wolf Song, Medicine Song, Bread Song and Farewell Song are all of much significance, indeed so much so that a large amount of space could well be devoted to this subject as to that of the dances.

In 1836 the Iowa were assigned a reservation in north-eastern Kansas, having two years previous ceded all their lands in Missouri. A portion of the tribe later moved to another tract in Oklahoma allotted to them in severalty in 1890, the surplus acreage being opened to settlement by the whites.

Prominent ethnographically and of equal

interest, being in many respects a typical Plains tribe, is the third to be mentioned in some detail, viz. the Pawnee or Pani, the word, according to Hale, being the same though of different orthography. This is a Confederacy of the Caddoan family. Their name is derived from the word *paŕiki*, meaning horn, so designated because of the peculiar method, entirely their own, of dressing the scalp-lock, the hair being stiffened with various substances such as fat and paint and thus made to stand erect or with a curve after the fashion of a horn.

This conclusion as to the name, however, is really one of conjecture rather than positive fact. Both Pani and Pawnee are terms applied quite broadly to Indian slaves, and it was a practice among both the French and English during the early periods of contact with the Indians to obtain from friendly tribes such captives as were taken in war and sell them among the white settlers as menials, this traffic being recognised in Canada as late as 1709 and so recorded in Charlevoix. Hence the theory put forward that because of the part taken in such trade the Pawnee became thus specifically named. They called themselves Chahiksichahiks, "men of men."

Their earliest history, or more properly the earliest historic mention of the tribe is that made in 1541, when they were described to Coronado by "the Turk," presumed to have been a Pawnee, who directed the adventurer to the province of Quivira, famous at the time for its fabulous riches. De Soto, too, writes of the "Apane" or "Quipana," at the same period, though whether these Indians were the true Pawnee or not will remain doubtful. Tonti, La Harpe and other French travellers mention their locality, but there is no proof that white men were among them before the latter half of the eighteenth century. Nevertheless they were known to settlers in the district of what is now New Mexico, fully one hundred years earlier.

Grinnell believes the Caddoan stock to have been originally in the south-west, probably as far as the shores of the Gulf of California, and their later history proves that they migrated in a north-easterly direction. They were the last to follow in the tide of wanderers from that section and their action was not as a compact body but slowly and in groups, without rapid progress and covering long periods of time. Tradition among the tribe tells of how they finally acquired the territory located for the most part in the valley

of the river Platte. Though this was not without
conquest, yet no mention is made of the con-
tending parties who may have been members of
the Shoshonean or Athapascan families or both,
as these peoples were trending toward the south
at about the same period. The Sioux, who
were, apart from the Algonquian, the only other
important family in those parts, tell of finding
the Pawnee on their arrival.

A curious fact may be referred to concerning
the geographic arrangement of the four most
prominent Pawnee tribes, from which a hint as
to the cause of the north-easterly movement may
be gleaned. The peculiar manner of grouping is
always observed: the Skidi chose the north-west
and were known as the "upper villages"; the
Pitahauerat were opposed to the first named, i.e.
always "down stream"; the Kitkehahki were
"up stream," while the Chaui were in the middle
or between the two last mentioned. For how
long a period they resided in the valley of the
Platte there is no definite knowledge, but it was
a sufficient time to give new terms to east and
west as applied to the eastwardly flowing river.

Because of the remoteness of this tribe from
the country early contested by the French and
Spanish, during the later seventeenth and early

eighteenth centuries, the Pawnee not only escaped the evil influences of white contamination but for a longer time retained their pristine customs and held their own in the matter of population and power. This was to be but momentary however as the ever advancing tide of human progress must sooner or later overtake even the most remote village. The later eighteenth century brought the final contact, introduced new diseases causing a corresponding decrease in population and, what may be considered equally important, loss of tribal power. When through the purchase of the Louisiana Territory, the Pawnee country passed under the control of the United States, these Indians came in close touch with the great trading centres in and about St Louis. Through the parts that they occupied at this time ran the great trading trail to the south-west and later that one which crossed the continent, and the constant travel as well as occasional settlement brought many changes and customs with which they were totally unfamiliar. Be it said to their lasting honour, that through all these vicissitudes and until the nineteenth century, the tribe has never made war upon the United States though provocation has been in some instances far from lacking.

Treaties between the Pawnee and the American Government have been numerous, extending from the first in 1818 until 1857. In 1876 they removed to Oklahoma and their history since that time has been that of common reservation life, which is to say, the abandonment of ancient custom. Since 1892, when they took their lands in severalty, they have become citizens of the United States.

Both in the matter of culture and in their physical make-up the Pawnee differ but little from the Sioux. Of a strong physique like their neighbours, their features are of a somewhat finer cast, the lips thinner and the lower part of the face more delicately chiselled. In general they are mesocephalic with some tendency towards brachycephaly. (Deniker.) The matter of inheritance seems to have been in the male line and they were divided into kinship groups distinguishable by totems. Tribes were likewise divided into more or less independent bands, and the leadership among these seems to have been more strongly developed than among surrounding tribes.

Traditions tell of a time when a woman was their chief. Within the period of recorded history, however, this office has been hereditary

in the male line and the power of the leader seems
to have been more absolute than was usual.

To an extent somewhat greater than common
the Pawnee engaged in agriculture. Individual
families planted and cultivated and crops of
pumpkins, beans, squashes and corn were generally abundant. Corn was considered sacred,
being termed "mother," and religious ceremonies
attended the planting, hoeing and harvesting.

The organisation among the tribes was based
on village communities representing subdivisions.
Each had its name and shrine containing the
sacred objects, and priests who had these in
charge. These men also had charge of the
rituals and ceremonies, though all authority
connected with social matters was relegated to
the head chiefs who were expected to give freely,
and who were usually surrounded by numerous
dependents. Such chiefs had their own heralds
who proclaimed orders or other matters of
interest to the tribes.

The potent factors holding the tribe together
were two: Ceremonies pertaining to the common
cult in which each village had its share, and the
tribal council composed of chiefs of the various
villages. So too was the Confederacy united,
the great council being composed of the councils

of the tribes. In such meetings strict rules of decorum and precedence were observed, none being entitled to a voice except they have the right to a seat, though a few of the privileged men were often permitted as spectators. This council determined all matters pertaining to tribal welfare or that of the Confederacy.

Religion among the Pawnee, while differing but slightly from that of the Sioux in ceremony, seems to have been of a somewhat more elaborate character and to it much more time was given both by individual and tribe as a whole. A study of the subject reveals the fact that the dominant features were to be found in the heavenly bodies and the cosmic forces, chief among which was Tirawa, or Atius Tirawa, known as "father" or "spirit." The elements as wind, rain, thunder and lightning were his messengers, while among the Skidi the morning and evening stars were masculine and feminine representatives connected with living forms on earth. For example, ceremonies concerning the bringing of primal life and the continual increase thereof began with the first thunder of spring, ending with human sacrifice at the period of the summer solstice, though the series of formal ceremonies did not cease until the harvesting of the mother corn in

the late autumn. The numerous religious formalities were accompanied at each stage by
certain shrines or "bundles," each of which was
in charge of an hereditary priest or keeper, though
it may be mentioned in passing that the office
was open at all times to proper aspirants.
Through the use of the sacred rituals it was
believed that a medium of communication was
possible between the supernatural powers and
the people, by which long life, prosperity and
above all food might be obtained. Only with
difficulty and at a comparatively recent date
have the human sacrifices been abolished.

The mythology of the Pawnee and indeed of
the whole Caddoan group is especially rich in
symbolism and poetic fancy, hence the somewhat elaborate religious system. Each tribe
possessed several sacred societies connected generally with a belief in supernatural animals. The
functions of these were to heal disease and to call
the game for the huntsman as well as dispense
occult powers. Their rites were occasionally
most dramatic in action as well as novel in
conception.

The matters pertaining to war were important. Parties gathered for this purpose were
almost invariably composed of volunteers in

cases of aggressive action and were in-
structed by some individual of the tribe. In
case of defence, however, the warriors fought
under their chief or some recognised leader.
The hunting of the buffalo, on the other hand,
was a tribal matter, and parties for this purpose
were led by officially appointed officers who
maintained law and order and supervised the
proper distribution of meat whereby each family
received its proper share.   Possibly no animal of
the Plains meant so much to the Pawnee as did
this one. It clothed as well as fed him and
furthermore was sacred; the hide both kept him
warm as clothes and housed him as a tipi, and
though not receiving an equal reverence with the
mother corn it was yet more highly respected.
The skull, typifying force and power, surmounted
many a lodge, and the buffalo of mythology
was a peculiarly potent medicine.

The artifacts of the tribe were confined mostly
to certain forms of pottery, basketry and weaving.
Houses of the more substantial kind were of earth,
their construction usually being accompanied by
forms of religious ceremony, one peculiar feature
of which was the anointing of the dwelling posts,
performed by a family upon returning to their
home after a protracted absence.

The custom of shaving the head prevailed among the men. The tonsure extended over the whole skull except for a narrow ridge from the forehead to the scalp-lock, the hair remaining in an erect position like a horn as previously described. A scarf was occasionally tied about the head in the manner of a turban.

Although tattooing was practised but little, the beard and eyebrows were plucked. The dress among the men consisted of a breech-cloth and moccasins; women generally wore a sleeveless leather gown terminating just below the knees and belted at the waist. From the waist hung small chains or leather thongs attached to which were the knife, sewing bag and often the fire steel. The women's moccasins were beaded or plain according to circumstances. Leggings were worn and robes used by both sexes in cold weather or on gala occasions. Face painting was common.

After marriage a man lived with his wife's family and polygamy was not uncommon. In every instance however descent was traced through the mother.

This important Plains tribe has dwindled greatly since the coming of the white man. Their historiographers as well as missionaries, Messrs

Allis and Dunbar, estimated their number at no less than ten thousand souls in 1838, a report which was generally substantiated by other authorities at about the same date. In 1849 nearly one-fourth of the number were swept away by cholera, and in the official report of six years since there was recorded 649 souls.

An estimate of the total number of Indians of Caddoan stock is 2000 at the present time.

A general summary of the foregoing chapter leads to some striking conclusions as to the inhabitants of the great prairie regions of America. Some of the more salient facts concerning three representative tribes have been dealt with and those features considered most important in each division are meant to serve as a somewhat detailed record of the life histories and cultural habits of these three great Indian families selected from nearly threescore. It will be observed that many traits are inherent to the race, that the Indian is indeed far from negative in character, and that his modes of thought vary little though his habitat may show extremes, and, barring climatic conditions, he is an Indian wherever found. The following chapter will show, nevertheless, certain differences, which, while non-racial in many respects, will shed a somewhat different light on these peoples.

A few words as a conclusion referring to these three several stocks may not be amiss. The Algonquian, a title taken from the name of the tribe so designated, originally occupied a greater amount of territory than any other on the American continent north of Mexico, their area extending from the north-eastern Atlantic coast to the Rocky Mountains and again south-east to Pamlico Sound, an inlet on the Atlantic coast in the State of North Carolina. Powell estimated thirty-six tribal divisions in 1887, though it was later found difficult to discriminate between tribes and villages, especially throughout New England. Mooney and Thomas assign a somewhat different classification, dividing the family into western, northern, north-eastern, central and eastern sections.

Anthropometric measurements prove the Algonquian to be tall, averaging 173 cm., with heavy, and, in the men, somewhat hooked noses, which are flatter in the women, and heavy cheek bones. The central tribes are almost brachycephalic. It may further be noted that the Cheyenne were even taller than the average.

As a linguistic stock they number to-day

about ninety thousand, one-half being in British America, the remainder in the United States. The largest of these tribes comprise the Chippewa and Cree in Canada.

Second to the Algonquian in size, and like them in deriving their family from their tribal name, comes the Siouan linguistic family. The meaning of Sioux, taken from the French Nadowessioux, itself a corruption from the Chippewa Nadowe-is-iw, is snake in the broad sense, thence metaphorically "enemy." The largest and best known tribal Confederacy, the Sioux, gives the name to the stock. They are known quite generally, however, as the Dakota, Lakota, or Nakota among themselves, and the various names by which the family, tribe and stock have been known from earliest times are numerous.

Their original habitat extended roughly from the west bank of the Mississippi northerly from the Arkansas almost to the Rocky Mountains, and certain bands also occupied territory east of the river first named for a short distance toward the Great Lakes. To the north they reached as far as the present Province of Saskatchewan in the Dominion of Canada. A second and in some respects a separate group were located in portions of North and South Carolina and Virginia, while a third division composed of the Biloxi were as far south as the Gulf of Mexico. Seven distinct sections are noted by Swanton and Thomas, and again, according to Powell, thirty-six tribal divisions are enumerated.

According to Deniker, who quotes ten Kate, Boas and others, the Siouan stock are as a rule tall (exceeding 1 m. 70), with a cephalic index of 79·8 in living subjects. Compared with the Indians of the western coast their features are strong, with prognathous jaw and prominent nose, the heads in no way being deformed and the stock as a whole showing fine examples physically of the American Indian type.

Based upon reports of both the Canadian and United States Indian Offices the total number of individuals composing this family to-day is approximately 40,800.

There is still some doubt among American ethnologists as to whether the Caddoan linguistic family properly includes the Pawnee. Gallatin, one of the foremost investigators and first among the students of the subject in his day (1836), regarded the two as distinct; investigation may prove the contrary. Usage as a family name, however, came from a Caddo word or term Ka'-ede or Kä'dohädä'cho, signifying "chief" according to Gatschet, and Caddo proper or "real Caddo" according to Miss Fletcher.

Geographically they may be referred to as the northern, middle and southern tribes, occupying a like number of localities, the first wholly surrounded by the Siouan family and located in portions of what is now Dakota, the middle, farther south and in the present States of Nebraska and Kansas, and the southern scattered about the region of the Red river of Louisiana and its tributaries in Arkansas and southern Oklahoma.

Physically the Pawnee are not unlike the Sioux. Strongly built, they have a somewhat finer cast of features with thinner lips and more delicate lines in the lower face.

CHAPTER V

To the student of ethnic conditions the differences between the Indians of the extreme south-western portion of the United States and those of the Plains and Atlantic coast are considerable. As Dorsey has said, "If we may better understand civilised man of to-day by a knowledge of man in more primitive conditions, then surely the South-west forms a field, not only to scientific students but to all who have a broad interest in mankind, second to that presented by no other region in the world."

This appellation "The South-west," must however appear to many to be somewhat ambiguous. The great arid stretches occupying parts of several States north of the Mexican border and touching upon California to the west, including a portion of Texas to the south-west, and with Nevada, Utah and Colorado to the north may roughly designate the territory covered, viz., from 30° to 40° north latitude and 100° to 120° west longitude.

Within this region, with an approximate area of 200,000 square miles, there are represented at the present time no less than nine linguistic stocks and about forty-five tribes divided for convenience of distinction into Pueblo and non-Pueblo peoples. Scattered through the whole section are thousands of ruins, even now for the most part unclassified. These, while of extraordinary interest to the archaeologist, can be touched upon here only in a cursory manner.

Those of the Pueblo group are in part comprised in the Keresan, Tanoan, Shoshonean (Hopi) and Zunian families; the non-Pueblo group includes the Athapascan, Piman and Yuman. Thus it is seen that two, the Athapascan and Shoshonean, out of five of the largest linguistic stocks of the continent, are represented in this district. Why the great Athapascan family, whose original habitat is the extreme north-west, should have, in part, migrated to the south will be explained in what follows.

The name Pueblo, of Spanish origin, meaning town or village, was first applied by the early conquerors and explorers from Spain who advanced northward out of Mexico, and has since been retained. Not only are the natives of these parts referred to as Pueblo peoples, but the

culture likewise is the "pueblo culture" and the
whole country is known as the "pueblo area."
Strictly speaking these tribes, as against those
known as the non-Pueblos, are confined to a strip
the eastern extent of which is in south-east
Arizona, thence south by east to the Rio Pecos
in New Mexico and south from Taos on the Rio
Grande to about El Paso in Texas. Originally,
as proved by archaeological investigation, they
continued to the far south, mingling with the
northern Aztec in Mexico.

The history of the first white invasion into
this wonderful region is fraught with unusual
interest. From the first the charm of the country
attracted the adventurer and explorer, and following closely upon those who entered the field for
glory came the soldiers of fortune lured by
wondrous tales or by the greed for gold. The
Spaniard Cabeza de Vaca, a survivor of the ill-
fated expedition of Narvaez in 1528, had brought
the news to Mexico. As the result a Franciscan,
Fray Marcos of Niza, travelling northward from
Mexico City in 1539, came upon the first recorded
peoples, the Zuni. He was foremost in sighting
the famed Seven Cities of Cibola, now identified
with the Zuni villages of western New Mexico,
and of these he took formal possession in the

name of Spain. His reports give a wonderful, though probably somewhat exaggerated account of this marvellous country.

This account was greeted with enthusiasm among his comrades farther south and in 1540 another expedition made under his guidance resulted in that most memorable journey of Coronado which has been described in such masterly fashion by Winship. His forces were the first to explore the Hopi villages at Tusayan, the Grand Cañon of the Colorado, the vast buffalo ranges and the magnificent Rio Grande Valley, but were unfortunate in not attaining the hoped-for El Dorado.

The story of this remarkable march reads more like romance than reality. It is the primal record of Tiguex, of Quivira and Pecos, and of the bloody annals of Indian atrocities and Spanish inhumanity. It did result, however, in the establishment of Franciscan missions which to-day survive, although active work was not really begun before the seventeenth century.

Many other detailed accounts of early visits by the Spaniards to these parts are available. Three Franciscans under the escort of Chamuscado entered the Tigua country in 1581, but were slain soon after. Antonio de Espejo left San Bartolome in Chihuahua in 1582, and his itinerary is to be traced to-day without difficulty. The return was made by way of the Pecos river and, though grossly overdrawn, his report is of contemporary interest.

Close upon Espejo followed Castaño de Sosa in 1590, and eight years later the most important of all expeditions took place, that of Oñate, the true coloniser of New Mexico and the founder of Santa Fé.

The formal Memorial of Fray Alonso de Benavides, Custodian of the Franciscan Order, setting forth the condition of affairs in 1629, resulted in the coming of no less than thirty missionaries as well as the erection of monasteries, and from this period a more considerable if still fragmentary history of the native population has been evolved. Until 1696 a story of continual Indian uprising and consequent punishment by those who encroached seems to have been common, but from the beginning of the eighteenth century the Pueblo have been, with few exceptions, peaceably inclined toward the white man. To-day many have advanced, to some extent at least, toward civilisation.

Among the Pueblo tribes, as among those of north-eastern America, the gentile system exists.

The social organisation is composed of numerous clans and gentes in each tribe. These terms are here used to designate descent in the female or male line respectively. The numbers of clans vary greatly as is shown for example in the pueblo of Sia, which comprises possibly one hundred souls divided amongst sixteen existing clans. Besides these there were originally twenty-one additional which are now extinct. There is also among the Pueblo, especially the Hopi, evidence of the phratral grouping of these clans, and even further evidence that a religious chief or priest presided over each.

Names of the clans were mostly taken from the elements or surrounding natural objects as plants or animals, these frequently being sub-divided into seasonal or regional groups, depending generally on the habits, or it may be said habit, of the chosen plant, animal, object or element; also to a certain extent on religious belief.

The status of women among the tribes of this section is generally higher than among the Plains Indians. These tribes are also monogamist. Tribes reckoning descent through the mother assume the home to be the property of the woman, and the marriage of a daughter brings the son-in-law to her house. Little ceremony is given to the marital arrangements and divorce is equally simple, it being within the wife's power to dismiss her husband for a trifling cause. She returns to her parents and is free to marry again. But cases are not infrequent which exhibit the utmost constancy, the couple remaining for life in perfect accord.

The division of labour among the men and women is as evenly arranged as circumstances will permit. Unlike many of their brethren of a more northern clime the men among the Pueblo help in the heavier domestic work. Women perform all the household duties and often help in the lighter farm work, particularly during times of harvest.

The gardens are also the property of the women who attend to the cultivation, carrying of water, etc., and it may be added that the making of pottery is strictly within their sphere. The offspring, in most pueblos at least, belongs to the clan of the mother; in the case of a family separation the children remain with the mother.

The government of the pueblos was originally in the hands of the priesthood. Representative societies regulated war and peace, witchcraft,

hunting and other functions pertaining to organisation. But on the coming of the Spaniard these
formalities were changed, at all events to outward
appearance, by the institution of a sort of elective
system established for the control of civil affairs,
the nearest approach to which may be found in
the present American form of government with
Governor and Lieutenant, Aldermen and others.
Except among the Hopi this system prevails
everywhere to-day, while the religious affairs and
those of a ceremonial nature only are controlled
by the priests.

Comparatively little of this ceremonial religion, or even mythology, has been recorded thus
far apart from Zuni, Hopi and Sia. Among the first-
named are a large number of organisations consisting of secret orders with functions pertaining
to war, hunting, magic and the like into which
the religious *motif* enters largely. A noticeable
fact is the use of the cardinal points, each of
which, according to Cushing, represented a
distinct religion. Instances are noted by this
writer, as the Pihlakwe or Bow Society among
the Zuni representing the west; Shumekewe, the
east; Newekwe, the upper region; Chitolakwe,
the lower region, and so on. Likewise each
society has its individual rites and ceremonies,

some performed in public and others in secret. The ritual dances performed in public are often elaborate as well as impressive.

The origin of the mythology of these tribes and of their secret organisations is most complicated, so much so that a mere outline of it here would be too lengthy for admission. Their artifacts are important. The "pueblo culture" as exhibited throughout this whole territory is such as to warrant the application of the term, yet there are many differences to be noted and especially in the architecture which may be the result of both environment and influence.

For example; the cliff-dwellings, used by the remote ancestors of the present occupants and found in the most northerly section of the Pueblo country, may be defined as the remains of dwellings actually built in walls of the cañons or cliffs, though in some cases advantage was taken of natural cavities made habitable by enlargement. It is conjectured that domiciles of this character were built primarily for the purpose of defence. The structural arrangement of dwellings varied accordingly throughout the valley or on the mesa tops, or plateaus. Sandstone, readily available, was most generally used together with the soft volcanic rock or tufa. In the southern

valleys however, bordering the Gila and Salt
rivers, the adobe or unburnt brick house of the
Mexicans is most common.

Before the advent of the Spaniard and consequently of the horse or donkey, methods of trans-
port formed a serious problem among the Pueblo.
Hence the somewhat limited use of timber which
would have to be brought from a distance.
Therefore arose a form of architecture brought
about in great part because of circumstances.
Compact in form, with many small rooms, the
dwellings were usually of several storeys. As a
rule no fixed plan was followed in laying out
a village, though the rectangular form, with open
courts seems to be most prevalent, additions
being made when necessary and these occasionally
influenced as to situation by the direction of the
sun, the result often showing groups of houses
either irregularly oblong, circular or semi-circular,
and even elliptical as to ground plan, with many
wings and minor projections. The pueblos of
early date were built to a large extent on the
principle of modern terraces, roofs of some of the
lower houses, for example, sufficing as a sort of
promenade or yard in front for the house next
above. Another feature of those first built, and
quite unlike the modern structure, is the fact

that the entrance was usually by ladder to the second storey, or by means of a hatchway or opening in the roof.

It is doubtful if chimneys were used before the coming of the white man. Originally fire-places were formed from a shallow box or by digging a pit in the middle of the floor, the smoke following a natural draught through the hole or entrance way in the roof as seen to-day in some of the kivas or "hot rooms" of the Hopi. Corner fireplaces were also in use, but dome-shaped ovens, shutters or even panelled doors were introduced much later.

Pieces of stone plastered with adobe mortar or the stones alone were used for flooring, the walls and ceilings being likewise of plaster similar to that used on the outside. The houses were owned by the women and for the most part constructed by them.

Among their arts may be included a good quality of basketry which, if not equal to some wrought by the tribes of California, was distinctive in itself and excellently woven, and generally ornamented with dyes derived from native substances now for the greater part superseded by the more ordinary commercial article. The skill shown by the Pueblo in weaving has not been excelled by any tribes north of Mexico, nor have they as potters been surpassed in the northern area. Their pottery consisted of every known form of utensil, from the large storage and cooking vessels to the elaborately painted and modelled bottles, ladles, bowls and platters as well as delicate jars and vases. Nor should the box-shaped receptacles be forgotten.

As workers in the soil these peoples, especially those of the northern area, must be classed more among horticulturists than agriculturists. Their methods were highly intensive. Irrigation from streams or reservoirs assisted them in their small fields of corn and cotton, the former being the chief crop, though the cotton was used extensively in their every-day clothing and traded quite considerably among surrounding tribes.

With the introduction of the sheep by Europeans the weaving of native wool became an industry of importance, and it is said that a woman of the Pueblo first brought the art among the Navaho, indeed many so-called "Navaho blankets" are in reality the product of Hopi and Zuni looms.

Touching their food-products again it may be remarked that the Pueblo of the south are given to a somewhat more elaborate system of tilling the

soil. Here extensive irrigation arrangements were
perfected and utilised by whole communities who
joined in the production of wheat, pumpkins and
melons, in addition to corn and onion patches.
Small home gardens are to-day cultivated under
the watchful care of the women.

The clothing of both sexes differs at present,
for obvious reasons, from that of the early inhabitants, though the breech-cloth is usually worn
by men now as formerly. The ancient dress consisted of a short tunic of deer skin with trousers of
the same material ending at the knees. Leggings
of cloth or skin covered the rest of the leg and
were held in place by garters and the moccasins
were of deer skin. A close fitting cap, well venti-
lated and decorated with feathers, was worn by the
warriors, and this is still used by the priest of the
Bow, at Zuni. Evidence has been produced showing the use of yucca fibre, as well as of feathers
and cotton in early times. Sandals of yucca fibre
were worn at one time instead of moccasins.

Among the men the hair is cut straight across
the forehead hanging usually an inch or a trifle
less from the eyebrow. Similarly it is cut horizontally at the neck line, the back hair being
gathered and tied behind. The ancient head-band
has given way to the bandana handkerchief except

among the Pueblo of the Rio Grande Valley,
where, unless on ceremonial occasions, the hair
is worn in side plaits, the band therefore not
being required. To-day the skin tunics and
trousers of the men are largely replaced by the
cheap cotton articles of the trader. Rabbit and
wild cat skins twisted in strands were formerly
used in cold weather as bedding or blankets, but
the bright coloured robes of native yarn or wool
are now commonly used for both the purposes
mentioned, and worn on gala occasions.

Ornamentation among the males consisted for
the most part of necklaces of ground and drilled
shell and turquoise beads, and ear and neck
pendants of the same material. Among the
women, necklaces, pendants, bracelets, earrings
and finger-rings of silver were used. The girls,
especially among the Hopi, wear ear-pendants
made of small tablets ornamented with turquoise
mosaics. Both copper and German silver are at
times used for ornamentation, but are not very
greatly prized among the Pueblo of either sex.
The art of working in these metals came from
Spanish craftsmen.

The costume of the women to-day consists of
a woollen dress to the knee, woven by natives and
usually in the form of a blanket, the ends being

sewn together and worn over the right and under the left shoulder. This is belted at the waist with a long woven, coloured sash, fringed and tucked in. In addition a shirt of cotton extends to the knees. Leggings are worn out of doors and consist of an entire deer skin wound continuously from the knee to the ankle and forming a part of the moccasin. These are not dyed as with the men. For indoor use leggings of knitted yarn are used.

Added to this apparel the women wear a light-weight cotton mantle, and in cold weather the customary blanket in the form of a shawl. The "ceremonial" blanket, embroidered, knotted and fringed, and made of white cotton, is a most valued possession.

Among the married women the hair is cut into a slight fringe in front, carefully parted in the middle and gathered in two huge coils behind the ears. Girls on reaching the marriageable age have the hair arranged in two large whorls on each side of the head, representing among the Hopi squash blossoms; these are symbols of fertility. Among certain tribes, however, the women of the Pueblo do not wear a fringe, though the hair is parted in the middle and worn in a braid on each side.

At a former period hunting was indulged in

among these tribes though to no great extent.
Deer, antelope and mountain lion as well as bear
were the game sought, and the eastern tribes
followed the buffalo on the plains. A few skilled
hunters are to be found to-day, but at present
rabbits seem to be the staple among mammals.
These are followed with sticks or trapped as are
other small game and birds, including eagles, the
latter being especially prized for the feathers.
Fish and certain animals are strictly tabooed as
food. Records prove that at one time large
flocks of turkeys were kept much as sheep and
goats are at present. They are still occasionally
to be found domesticated as are eagles, for their
plumage. Dogs are plentiful but not used as
among other tribes for beasts of burden. Horses
came with the white man, also the horned cattle
and sheep. A species of large animal not unlike
the llama in appearance has been noted in picto-
graphs and figurines discovered in southern
Arizona. These were evidently herded by men
using the bolas, thus disproving statements that
this weapon was only used by the South Americans and Eskimo.

Statistics relating to the population of the
Pueblo are not satisfactory. External evidence
shows that little variation as to numbers has

occurred in the last two centuries, and to-day there are possibly 8000 souls in thirty-six pueblos, not including the Hopi of Arizona nor the Piro and Tigua of Texas and Chihuahua. Reports emanating from various sources have existed on the subject since 1630, many of the early ones being exaggerated and others mere guesswork.

Very different not only in customs and manners, but using a wholly dissimilar language, are the peoples classified as the non-Pueblo. Occupying the same desert region and in many respects surrounded by like environment these brothers in locality only prove by their linguistic characteristics to be intruders who have become acclimatised. A study of their culture shows them to be nomads and not indigenous,—wanderers from a distant part who seemingly preferred the southland to their primal home, and whom study has shown to be members of distinct and independent stocks as the Athapascan, Shoshonean and others. Three tribes as typical examples are chosen, the Navaho, Mohave and Apache.

In general among this last group, or non-Pueblo Indians, a vast difference is first to be discerned in their manner of living. Instead of the substantial and often carefully constructed houses comprised within the compact villages of the Pueblo, there is to be found little or in some instances no village life whatever. Rude, and often but temporary, shelters are scattered about the country, families of different tribes being found in one part or another, the dwellings at best being mere shacks in summer and hardly more durable or desirable in the winter season.

Again, agriculture, while practised, is by no means brought to the art it is among the Pueblo. The making of baskets has been highly developed, yet on the other hand the arts in general are in scant evidence and the women make but little pottery. Even the garments undergo a change among these tribes who wear at present, instead of woven garments often of beautiful texture, buckskin which in turn has been substituted for a scanty costume of shredded bark.

Furthermore, a difference occurs in the religion. There is still a seriousness but the incentive is more properly the medicine-man soothsayer than the priest and there is a noticeable lack of such accompanying ceremony as exists among the more sedentary tribes.

For the most part the habitat of the non-Pueblo to be described below is directly to the west of the tribes first treated. Inasmuch as the

"south-west" may include a large part of
California and extend to the Pacific, it is well
to define somewhat the area, if it be but roughly,
of the tribes noted, though none of them actually
belonged to or are situate to-day in any part of
Californian territory.

Were it possible to give even the remotest
idea as to the cause of the separation of the
Navaho and Apache from their parent stock the
Athapascan of north-eastern Canada, a story
long sought and well worth recounting would be
eagerly read by all students of American ethnology. Linguistics prove the relationship. The
migration from the district of the Mackenzie river
and northern shores of the Great Lakes to the
arid country of the south must have been made
under conditions more or less strenuous, though
it would appear that neither tribe suffered to any
great extent in the southerly flight. On the
contrary, for centuries the warlike desperadoes
have been a menace and trial to the more peaceful
tribes occupying adjacent parts and the story
of the Apache is one of continued strife and
depredation. Their record, therefore, will be
first narrated.

So many tribal groups are to be found among
these Indians that it is often difficult to determine

which are being referred to by various writers. The early forays and conquests of the Apache assisted largely in absorbing a considerable outside element, notably Piman, Yuman and Spanish stock, despite the fact that intermarriage in this way broke clan ties.

Among the divisions more commonly accepted may be included the Coyoteros, consisting of the White Mountain and Pinal groups; the Querechos, among whom were the Mescaleros, Jicarillas, Faraones, Llaneros and no doubt the Lipan; Chiricahua; Pinalenos; Arivaipa; Gila Apache embracing the Gilenos, Mimbrenos, Mogollones; and the Tontos. As late as 1903 these divisions were rearranged somewhat, under official care. There are probably 6000 of the tribe surviving to-day on various reservations or under charge of agents.

The name Apache is undoubtedly of Zuni origin and from the word *ápachu* meaning "enemy." The tribes collectively referred to under this name form the most southerly group of the Athapascan family and speak of themselves as the N'de, Dïnë, Tinne, Tïnde or Inde, meaning "people," and this they have in common with the great northern family from which they sprung.

All evidence seems to prove that those of the

south were not so numerous at an early date as now, and the presumption has been that the increase comes from foreign admixture. From measurements among them by Dr Hrdlička, the foremost American physical anthropologist, it would seem, on the contrary, that there is unusual freedom from outside blood. Be this as it may their number has increased largely since the beginning of the seventeenth century.

Oñate, in 1598, seems to be the first to mention the Apache. Coronado has a statement referring to the Querechos as early as 1541, and this tribe is probably the Vaqueros of Benavides, though it is not known that they were as far west as Arizona until the latter part of the century.

From the beginning until late years these Indians have been noted for their fierce and war-like disposition. It may be safely said that none of the Indians north of the Mexican border have given the United States more trouble. Their history for the last 100 years is one of bloodshed and murder, particularly since the advent of their medicine-man and prophet the late Geronimo or Goyathlay (one who yearns) in 1877.

The Jicarilla tribe of northern New Mexico may be mentioned first as being representative. Stock raising and basket making are the important

industries among them on their reservation of
416,000 acres. There are three bands each with
its chief under a head chief chosen by joint
vote. All Indians are gamblers more or less, but
these people are inveterate; gaming principally
with cards or by pitching quoits, though playing
the latter game in a manner peculiarly their own.
With the Jicarilla as with other Apache the
favourite drink is "tiswin" made from fermented
corn and used in large quantities. Both men
and women smoke incessantly.

It is said that among these Indians as with
the southern Ute of Colorado, secret disposal of
the dead is common. A wealthy man or chief
may practise polygamy. A child at birth is
given the name of some important event happen-
ing at the time and this name is known only to
itself and its parents until the time of marrying,
on which occasion the second party to the con-
tract also shares the secret. The performance of
marriage as with many other south-western tribes
is somewhat lightly considered. Son-in-law and
mother-in-law never speak.

In eating, pork is strictly tabooed. Witchcraft is still to be found among them, medicine-
men being resorted to in illness. There are few
dances among the band, their principal one

occurring in the spring.   The usual habitation is a tent.

Passing further to the west are to be found the White Mountain and San Carlos bands in Arizona, and more centrally located in New Mexico, the Mescalero, the latter numbering about 450 on a reservation containing 475,000 acres of which but a comparatively small part is adapted to cultivation.   Mountains stern in their ruggedness or thickly covered with cedar and pine, fir and oak, abound throughout the whole section, and it is in the intervening valleys fed by springs and with numerous flowing streams that the land lends itself to pasture and where are to be found in abundance deer, antelope and wild turkey.   While the Mescalero own horses and cattle, little attention is paid to farming, and their main revenue is derived from the manufacture of willow baskets which are sold to collectors or traded with the Mexicans in large numbers.   Two clans, each with its chief, prevail in the tribe.   Ceremonial dances are held frequently, some of four days' duration, but among this band the medicine-man has lost his hold. At death all personal property belonging to the deceased is burned.   With rude aboriginal ideas concerning religion there now exists among them

much outside formality which has been incorporated, especially that from Mexican sources.
Though originally a most intractable people the
Mescalero have at last come to realise the in-
evitable necessity of submission.

The Arizona Apache, situate at this time upon
the White Mountain and San Carlos Reservations
in that State, are more numerous and in many
respects better known than their neighbours.
This reservation, containing 2,528,000 acres, is
ninety-five miles in length from north to south
and seventy miles wide.   In the north-central
section the Salt river drains the adjoining parts
with numerous tributaries emptying into the Gila,
many of which are fed by the melting snows of
the surrounding mountain ranges.   The banks
of these streams when irrigated produce abun-
dantly.   Numerous bands are to be found en-
camped along such waterways where trout are
usually plentiful, and there is little difficulty in
procuring deer, bear and wild turkey.   Petty
chiefs rule the camps and there are altogether
about 4500 Indians included in the Agency.

As distinguished from his brethren of the race
the Apache has been looked upon as exceptionally
ferocious.   This unenviable reputation might be
modified somewhat, and it should be said that the

whole ought not to be judged entirely by the exception. Such traits were indeed cultivated by certain tribes as the Indian Office Reports show, but it would be unfair to ascribe this character to all.

In stature they are similar to other natives of the region, and it is not uncommon to find well-proportioned men above six feet in height. Given somewhat to superstition they are at all times found to be timid and charms are quite frequently used. Beads of stone found among the ruined pueblos are looked upon as powerful protective agents; also beads of lightning-riven rocks or trees help in the cure of disease and forefend evil. In addition to these charms, others are to be purchased from medicine-men or obtained from graves, both being considered of great worth, though this fetish is not so prominent here as among the Pueblo tribes. Probably among the symbols of the Apache, the lightning, whose power they greatly revere, is most potent. The storm-cloud, as well as the four winds appearing from the four world-quarters, is likewise depicted.

The culture traits as also many of the manners and customs of this tribe will be described more fully than those of the others chosen, unless there be some distinct traits more noticeable among

either Mohave or Navaho, for the reason that the
latter may be better known as a whole and from
the fact that less detailed information is available
regarding the Apache than the other two tribes.
We shall therefore deal in what follows with the
subject in order from birth to death, thus giving
a rough idea of the character of this branch of
the south-western aborigines.

Very shortly after birth the Apache infant is
put into its crudely fashioned cradle, an article
made for the most part of slats or thin strips of
board having a hood or covering of the same
though lighter material. Once placed in this
cradle, custom has it that none other shall at any
time be occupied. Childhood in its numerous
phases differs but little here from childhood elsewhere.

Any young man endowed with proper natural
gifts may enter the ranks of the medicine-men,
among whom there seem to exist no fixed
doctrines or tenets. One exception as to living,
however, must be followed; they partake of no
intoxicants. Individuals follow their own in-
clinations and invent such symbols among
themselves as are apparently most needed or
are most eminently successful.

Among both men and women the custom of

tattooing is not infrequent. The forehead and often the chin are covered, generally with designs of geometric shape and usually dark blue in colour. It is not uncommon to trace the upper design as far downward as the tip of the nose.

In dress this branch of the non-Pueblos differs somewhat from the other tribes and especially in respect of the moccasins which have a hard sole with an upward curve at the toe, being so made for protection against the cacti and thorns of the region. Occasionally moccasins of the better quality are made with long uppers reaching in some instances to the thigh and thereby protecting the leg like a boot. The common variety has three or four folds of material bound about the lower leg and extending to the knee. Both kinds have hard usage; hence as the lower part becomes worn it is gradually brought down until often the new moccasin which reached the thigh ends by barely covering the ankle. Decoration of this article either by painting or the use of beads is not common. Those found thus gaudily arrayed are usually for the purpose of trade or sale.

An interesting article of apparel among the women, and one worn on ceremonial occasions, is the short buckskin waist or shirt, opened both back and front at the neck, and about the yoke of which beads of several colours are usually worked in various designs. A typical shirt might have below these a row, or two rows of tin pendants, and on the sides and often extending over the shoulders designs in red flannel heightened as to effect by an occasional brass button.

Skirts also of buckskin, worn by the women, are of considerable weight. These are often decorated in the same way with tin pendants and rows of fringe, and in some instances painted yellow with ochre. Tin pendants are likewise occasionally attached to the bottom of the fringes.

Necklaces are frequently worn by both men and women. These consist for the most part of many strands of beads, hanging loosely on the breast, though the flat compact band is not uncommon. Earrings of beads and bracelets of the same articles are worn by both sexes; others are made of iron, copper and brass wire. During later years maidens aspire to wear in their back hair a leather ornament made somewhat in the form of a figure eight and profusely decorated with large brass buttons. Feathers, usually from the eagle, were formerly used to a great extent by the men and attached by buckskin thongs to the hair or the hat. During the period of mourning the men cut the hair squarely around their heads.

Polygamy prevails among the Apache with certain restrictions. For example, a man who is able to do so marries his wife's younger sisters as rapidly as they mature or, in lieu of available relations, he marries among the same clan. If however he wishes to marry his brother's widow, he must do so within a twelvemonth else she is free to marry whom she will. Marriage by purchase is the usual form. To a certain extent the numerous bands have intermarried and there are a few Mexicans and white men to be found among them as husbands.

The industries of the tribe are not extensive, basket making being the principal one among the women. Two kinds are most in evidence, the bowl-like "tsa" and the sewed water-jug or "tus." These are made in coils of either willow or cotton-wood, the wrapping being in every instance of the latter material. Added to these are the burden baskets ornamented in colour, their bases being carefully protected by buckskin, and the water vessels made in the form of bottles from the bush of the squaw-berry. Needless to say these last are watertight, so made by coating with piñon gum. In some instances

the interstices are first filled in with crushed
cedar berries before sealing. A few other forms
are also to be had.

The important matter of food-stuffs must not
be overlooked. Among the meats the flesh of
the wild turkey and deer is the most common,
fishing birds being wholly tabooed. Corn and
melons are to be had in varying quantities and
so are edible acorns, sunflower seeds, willow buds,
as well as juniper berries and walnuts. Various
other berries, beans and mescal[1] are eaten, the last
used in several forms. While the flower stock of
the mescal is still tender the cabbage portion is
cut, placed under stone and heated, then covered
with bear grease and earth. Left thus for a day a
pulpy mass is finally secured containing a heavy
syrup; this portion is highly esteemed. This same
article crushed with ripe black walnuts diluted
with water forms a favourite dish. Again the
more fibrous portions of the mescal are bruised
and preserved in the form of cakes and stored
for future use.

Meat, with a side dish of squaw-berries, is
greatly relished.

The bow and arrow still obtains as a formidable
weapon among the Apache. Bows of from four to

[1] See note p. 153.

five feet in length are used with arrows of reed and a hard wood foreshaft, tipped with flint, chalcedony or obsidian. Quivers made from the skin of the mountain lion, the tail hanging from the bottom, are common as are also those of deer skin.

This weapon, together with the spear and war-club, is universal. A curious method of poisoning the arrows was to place the tip into the liver of a deer previously bitten by a rattlesnake. The war-club is reminiscent of early man in other parts and consists of a stone oval in shape and cased in raw hide to which the handle is attached. The spear is made of a long wooden shaft to which, by using the skin of a cow's tail, an iron blade not unlike a sword or bayonet may be affixed. Legend has it that "long time ago" the Apache wore about the waist lariats of horse hair, which were used to excellent effect in entangling an enemy.

The houses of these Indians are known as "campos" and are oval in shape, and as a rule are only sufficient in height to allow the occupant to stand erect in the centre. The construction is simple, poles being thrust into the ground and drawn together at the top around which are interlaced and twisted twigs and grasses. When obtainable, pieces of canvas or heavy cloth are often used as a covering. Such are the common forms, though a rectangular shape is sometimes found. This form of dwelling is used throughout the summer or pleasant seasons. In winter huts or houses made of heavier material are used and generally in the more wooded sections and away from the vicinity of fields and streams, water being procured from the melting snows.

Within the shelter of the campos are to be found the various household furnishings, few in number and stored in saddle-bags used for such purposes then and as packs when on the march. Blankets and skins used for bedding are folded when not needed. With large gourds for water and smaller ones for dippers, small circular stone mortars for preparing paints, upper and lower mealing stones for grinding coffee, berries, etc., and a fire drill, the household utensils are practically complete. The fireplace consists of a hole in the centre of the floor, the smoke escaping through an aperture above. To gather about the vessels and help themselves at will comprises the whole ceremony of eating.

In common with all other southern Indians and therefore it may be said with the rest of the race, the Apache, wherever found, is a born gambler. Women as well as men play. The former engage especially in what is called "tsay-dithl" or throw-sticks, and the men in "naashosh," a sort of ring and javelin game. Spanish playing cards are in common use.

There is a kind of social dance indulged in and enjoyed by both men and women. Apart from this, two others only are used, the Devil's Dance and the Medicine Dance, neither of which is of particular importance. Among their musical instruments may be catalogued the drum, and a sort of violin made from a hollow cylinder with a single sinew string and a small bow the strings of which are made from horse hair. Drums are usually improvised for the occasion and of simple construction, an old kettle or bucket forming the base over which is tightly stretched a piece of deer skin. The stick for beating these has a loop at one end.

Thus fares the life of these Indians from beginning to end. The bodies of adults are buried or deposited in clefts among the rocks, though in the latter case a considerable covering is used. Those of children, after being enveloped in clothing and blankets, are occasionally placed in trees, upon a platform made from branches and sticks. So much for the Indians collectively known as the Apache.

During 1857–58, Lieut. Joseph C. Ives, acting
under Government instructions, explored the
then little-known cañon of the great Colorado
river of the west. It would appear that he was the
first to call particular attention to the Mohave,
coming upon them originally as a few scattered
families in the Cottonwood Valley. Lieut. Ives
remarked at some length on the physique of
these peoples, especially the attractiveness of
their women, and since that time, in the light
of more careful investigation, little has been
found to refute his statements.

The term Mohave is derived from "hamok,"
meaning three, and "avi" mountain. The members of this tribe, now numbering about 1500,
athletic, strong and well developed, comprise
what was originally the most warlike and
populous of all the bands of the Yuman family.

According to A. L. Kroeber, who has made a
somewhat extended study of them, it would
appear that their tribal organisation is loose,
that "there is no full gentile system, but something closely akin to it, which may be called
either an incipient or decadent clan system."
It is also evident that the chieftainship was
hereditary in the male line. A curious consanguineal feature seems to be apparent in that

certain men and all their ancestors and descendants, in the male line, had one name only for all female relatives. This custom appears no longer to exist.

Among this tribe tattooing seems to be universal; indeed they are to-day famed for artistic work of this kind as well as for the painting of the body, though in the former case the work is confined to but small areas on the skin. Such art as is displayed in native manufacture seems to be limited almost solely to pottery wherein they show excellent judgment as well as patience and taste. Their products are crudely decorated and made up for the most part of bowls, dippers and ollas as among the Zuni. They contrive toy dolls of clay, displaying much ingenuity, the faces being painted and natural hair attached to the head. Miniature bead necklaces are also used on them. The beautiful beadwork and decorated bows and arrows that are offered for sale to-day are not to be confused with the handicraft of an earlier period.

Singularly enough though a river tribe, residing now as formerly on both sides of the Colorado, the Mohave constructed no canoes, resorting to rafts when necessary, or to balsas, a sort of conveyance made among themselves,

of reeds or rushes tied in bundles, usually if not
always with more or less approximation to a
boat of cigar shape.

Like the Apache, this tribe seems to have
had no large settlements, and if dwellings of any
sort were erected they were usually scattered.
Those used were low and generally of four sides,
supported by a like number of posts in the centre,
the walls being from two to three feet in height
with a flat roof of brush covered with sand.
Granaries, which were frequent, were cylindrical
structures covered in the same way.

As a whole the Mohave of to-day are industrious and universally generous. Shoes and
head-coverings are not common. They have
never been classed as hunters, their chief staples
of food being the articles cultivated such as corn
and melons and some wheat, added to which are
the pumpkins, beans, mescal and piñon nuts,
fish being used sparingly. Irrigation was not
practised and they relied on the inundation of
the lowlands for the needed moisture, hence an
uncertainty of annual crops.

From the foregoing it may readily be concluded that articles of skin and bone were
infrequent. The place of such materials was
taken by the use of various vegetable fibres and

portions of the inner bark of the willow.   Baskets were, and still are, in common use, obtained however from neighbouring tribes and not a native product.

Gambling is the most common vice.   Often, after an utter monetary loss, every article of wearing apparel is put at stake with imaginable results.   Thus it will be observed that in many respects there is little if any difference between the Indian as a member of Pueblo or non-Pueblo communities.

Cremation is usually resorted to as the last rite.

The majority of the Mohave are at present found on the Mohave or Colorado River Reservation.

Probably the best known, or at least the most widely mentioned, among the non-Pueblo of the south-west are the Navaho, located at this time on a reservation for the most part in Arizona and extending into north-western New Mexico and a small part of Utah, the largest of its kind within the borders of the United States, comprising nearly 10,000,000 acres or 15,000 square miles.

Infinitely barren and for the most part arid, their home is in the heart of the great American

desert, where the average rainfall is from ten to
fourteen inches during the short seasons, the
winters long and cold because of the high altitude
and the season of crops correspondingly short;
where Nature herself seems to have exhibited
her very vitals to the view of man.

The mighty cañons, titanic in their massive-
ness; the lava beds, upheavals of centuries,
expelled by some mighty power illustrative of
long-pent energy,—these inspire a sense of awful-
ness beyond comparison, as if all modesty had
been overlooked in the great disturbance and
Earth itself had become dismembered in this
vision of chaos.

Here then, among these erosions and these
tablelands or plateaus, live the Navaho, the
first record of whom is probably that of Oñate
in 1598, though they are first mentioned under
their present name by Zárate-Salmeron about
1629. Missionaries were among them during the
eighteenth century but to no effect.

In accordance with the best authorities this
important Athapascan tribe originated some 500
years since, though in reality they have among
themselves no positive story of their own
origin. Impressions gained from their legends
lead to the belief that they came first into the

south-west in small groups if not in families. Though linguistically classed as Athapascan their numbers include many accessions from various stocks as Keresan, Tanoan, Yuman, as well as Shoshonean, in consequence of which the Navaho of to-day are a most composite people. Proof of undoubted Athapascan affinity is shown by their vocabulary in its grammatical structure, this being both copious and intricate.

Further proof of their mixed origin is shown in the difficulty experienced in finding a prevailing type, the men varying in size from diminutive to above the average height; having strong features, aquiline noses and prognathous chins, from which they descend to the more subdued face of the Pueblo. The skulls are brachy- or hyperbrachy-cephalic, the result of the hard cradle board used in infancy, and in this they approach the Pueblo physically even more than do the Apache. It may further be mentioned that their faces, generally speaking, are more hirsute than those of the eastern nations, and that on the whole they are in appearance more pleasing and in-telligent than the average native. They seem to be without the common stoical manner, even given to jest and joviality among themselves. With this they couple an industry which is especially

commendable. According to the late Dr Washington Matthews, one of the foremost students
of the tribe, they are progressive especially as
stock-raisers, though less given to agricultural
pursuits because of the non-adaptability of the
region in which they dwell.

Since 1867 they have been prosperous and
undoubtedly have increased largely in numbers,
a census taken in 1900 estimating 28,500 souls.

The social organisations of the tribe are
interesting, fifty-one clan names having been
recorded, though the present number may be
somewhat less, two being wholly extinct and
several others nearly so. As among various
Plains Indians, these clans are in phratry groups
of which some authorities report eight and others
eleven. On the other hand there are those who
doubt the existence of any well-defined phratry
system. As the form implies, descent is in the
female line; the man belongs to his mother's
clan and in marrying takes a woman from without. Hence the women's social position is high
and they wield great influence, often being
possessors of considerable property in their own
right which is not alienated by marriage.

Until within the last quarter of a century the
belief was current that the Navaho had little in

the way of an established religious belief. Investigation has proved that the facts are quite to the contrary and that they are a highly religious people having numerous well-defined divinities as local gods, and animal and nature gods, and a vast mythic and legendary lore. Greatest among their many deities appears to be one, a goddess, known as Estsánatlehi, "Woman who Changes," "Woman who Rejuvenates Herself," according to translation, one who is never the same or becomes young or old at will. Dr Matthews considered this to refer to Mother Nature, an apotheosis of the changing year.

Added to the above are thousands of songs and prayers each significant in itself, formulated for special occasions and learned and repeated in the most precise manner. Again, experts have succeeded in noting in the numerous unusual musical compositions of the tribe much which bears distinct resemblance to our own modern forms of rhythm and style.

Many of the dance ceremonies among these Indians are of the utmost importance, some continuing through periods of ten days' duration and being participated in by men who have given years of study to the subject. Prominent features on such occasions are the pictures painted in dry powders on the floor of the medicine lodge and known as *dry paintings*. Space precludes writing at length on these subjects but all of this cultus is of undoubted antiquity.

The art of the Navaho is famous in at least one particular, that of weaving. Especially are they celebrated for their blankets which on account of their beauty and utility are much in demand by the traders, but added to these are the belts, garters and saddle girths, all products of the simple hand looms which have remained unchanged for generations. Legend says that at an early period this loom was unknown among them and that its use was taught by the Pueblo women brought into the tribe by capture. They claim, further, to have dressed first in skins or in mats made of a vegetable fibre, but be this as it may, none of the south-western tribes equal them at present as weavers. The few basket makers among the Navaho are descendants of some Ute or Paiute taken as prisoners at an early date. Because of the small numbers made, very few baskets can be acquired outside the tribe and among themselves these are used for the most part for ceremonial purposes. Furthermore, except for their own use, little pottery is made by the tribe, though originally they made an exceptionally fine red ware, decorated in black with typical designs.

The household utensils are simple. Corn is still ground by hand on the metate as are other grains, and for ceremonial use they continue to bake food in the ground and in other aboriginal ways.

There are silversmiths among the tribe who no doubt learned their art for the most part from the Mexicans, and they have adapted certain methods to their own environment. The Government training schools have wrought many changes in this art, as indeed in their methods of cookery, so that to-day the manners taught by civilisation are to a great extent prevalent, except as concerns weaving.

Among the Navaho the dwelling is termed the hogán, a simple structure though erected with much ceremony. It varies in style, the usual form being conical, and is built of sticks set on end and covered with grass, branches and twigs and finally with earth, the height often being too low to allow a man of ordinary stature to stand upright. It is necessary to bend on entering and the doorway consists of a sort of passage or miniature hall, the purpose of which

is not wholly evident.   The main room is without
a chimney, a hole in the roof allowing exit for the
smoke.   Hogáns partly of stone or of logs laid
horizontally are not uncommon, and in the
summer the ordinary lean-to or shed, or even
small enclosures of branches are frequently used
as habitations.   Sweat-houses are numerous as
among nearly all tribes, and with the Navaho
consist of small conical hogáns without an
opening at the apex, as fires are made outside
and hot stones put within by which means the
temperature is raised.

Medicine lodges are, on the contrary, hogáns
of considerable size.   When built in the region of
trees the roofs are flat, but latterly structures
of substantial stone, with windows, doors and
chimneys, are replacing the ruder efforts of the
past.

The foremost reason for building the somewhat flimsy residence, so much used until a
comparatively recent date, was on account of
a superstition prevalent then as now concerning
death.   Custom bade that the house in which a
person had died should be destroyed.   Such a
place was called a "chindi-hogán," or devil
house, and could never again be occupied.   To-
day those living in the more substantial homes

carry a dying comrade outside, thus saving the
house to posterity.

It has been said that none of the North
American tribes have greater dread of mortuary
remains, or of ghosts and their like, than have
the Navaho.

CHAPTER VI

Ordinarily, a sketch of the mythology of a people should include to a great extent its religion as well. Indeed in a large degree primitive religion is mythology, and the two if considered separately will often be found to originate in a common source. On the other hand, however, a study of myths must not be confounded with a more simple or more poetic element which, as an individual branch, has been termed folklore.

Let us consider therefore that myths for the present purpose among the aborigines of America exist in an intermediate position between religion, science and poetry, inasmuch as such a course will help to explain numerous phenomena while leaving much free to the imagination. Within such a range must be included animism, the belief in spiritual beings, though this is according to many writers widely synonymous with the religious motive. It is more or less difficult to write intelligently on a subject so complex without a word or two of explanation which at the best can hardly be called elementary.

If the North American tribes held to a definite system of ancestor worship, among their mythologies no support has thus far been found for such a belief. An infinite variety of myths is apparent, yet after all they may be reduced to a limited number of ideas and fancies, explanations of which, such as the origin of plants, animals, the earth, stars, and even man, become to a great extent simple if not childish and are on the whole founded on the animistic idea. The substance in most instances remains the same, though the nature of the country may change as well as the details, and borrowed myths are numerous among all peoples.

For example: the doctrine of the possession of immortal life applied to lifeless and mindless things, inanimate in the beginning but endowed by the myth-maker, may be as common a mode of procedure among the Déné of the north as among the tribes of the coasts surrounding the Gulf of Mexico. Hence animism may be selected to express what was considered an essential characteristic of a most complex institution. This then rather than a more potent form of ancestor worship supplies the basis of the mythology of the Indian. It presumed their opinions regarding the genesis, the history and the functions as well as destiny of themselves and their phenomena, and was the first principle of their past and present as well as their future.

As a further example germane to the subject: a savage myth is essentially an account of a humanised fictitious man or woman personifying some principle of nature or faculty of the mind, performing his or her function through the medium of magic power. Whether this personage be one of the elements, or a tree, rock, river or plant, it was thought of as being in human form and the possessor of will and power either for good or evil. A god or hero, evil spirit or devil, its action was significant and consideration was meted accordingly. For our present interest these myths are threefold in showing first their use as concerns the customs and art of the aborigines, second the development of the peoples through such channels, and third as a literary product and a wonderful story of persons and things. In that order therefore they will be developed.

The world as known to the Indian was not large. His ignorance of all things outside the horizon of his own wanderings aids the student

not a little, from the fact that the study may
have a formal limit, but even so it remains one
about which little has been written because of
lack of definite knowledge. Origin myths in
particular are universal and many are remarkable; yet in America, as elsewhere, the usual
difficulties are experienced.

From the narratives of this character it is
learned that an earlier world than the present
existed, and this was usually located above
the middle sky, having been there before the
beginning of time. Here dwelt the first or
prototypal personages resembling man and possessing all his attributes. The life of the Indian
to-day is patterned after this man-being of
the first estate. At a period still antedating
the advent of man upon this earth internal
strife changed the first state of tranquillity and
because of this commotion and collision a certain
faction was banished to earth. At this time
present appearances were assumed. There came
too animals, trees and plants, these likewise
having been in an earlier day man-beings with
the others.

Those who remained in the skyland were unchanged, in other words were immortal, separate
and peculiar unto themselves; their minds were

as in the beginning. Those who came to earth received what was required and what each nature demanded. They were in a transformed state what they had previously been in the world above.

These creation myths are numerous. Another represents the first men emerging from the earth, in the bowels of which they had previously existed until the world above was discovered by accident, and there are many descriptions of this, as also of the first theory, ably presented by students of the subject both in America and elsewhere. Yet this portion of Indian mythology forms a study in itself, the details of which are as yet but imperfectly understood. Obviously the Indian stood alone in creating his ideas. White men were unknown to the myth-makers as were all other men in regions not comprised within the American hemisphere. This first cycle, as Curtin aptly terms those myths referring to the creation, is followed by another devoted more especially to the changes occurring in natural objects, the "phenomena and processes as observed throughout nature" as he further defines it.

One important point to be brought out and of more than passing interest, before considering the second cycle, is the fact that certain areas disclose various and distinctive myths or groups of myths. As might be imagined, these to a greater or less extent coincide with the culture areas as designated on the linguistic map, such as the South-west, Plains, North-west Coast, etc. Yet the limits of these myth-sections are naturally less easily defined than are the clearly marked areas of culture, certain myth incidents having a much wider scope and some being readily extended from ocean to ocean or from the Gulf to the Arctic regions. It is plain that migration has largely influenced this condition, and, if the spreading of the Athapascan stock be taken as an instance, it can easily be understood why the Pueblo of New Mexico retain numerous traditions with the tribes of northern Canada, or the Cheyenne or Chippewa of the Plains have similar legends to those of the Cree or the Indians of eastern Canada. Myths have followed in the wake of migrations or even trade lines and in this way a wide dispersal can readily be accounted for. Again there are groups among whom the migratory myth is wholly unknown, others where it is considered foremost, and still others where it is noticed but dimly.

An idea even broader than this may be formulated if the substance of the myth be considered, but, *per contra*, the great difference between the Eskimo, for example, and the tribes farther south is doubly apparent though some of the legends and tales may often overlap or intertwine one with another. The Eskimo, however, is lacking in animal tales and his evident matter-of-factness is most noticeable when compared with almost any other family.

In its relation to known mythologies the American can be said to be associated only with those of north-eastern Asia where indeed the resemblance is most striking. North-western America and that part of Asia referred to form practically one group and this is the only clear relationship shown thus far with the outside world.

Instead of supplying what might be hastily considered a clue to the origin not only of the American Indian but his mythology as well, evidence as far as gathered proves that, on the contrary, the Asiatic tribes have been influenced by and have obtained from those of the western continent the bulk of their folk-stories and not the reverse. The influence has passed from America to Asia and belongs to a stage of culture which was undoubtedly possessed by the remote ancestors of the Indians of the present time.

In working out a logical plan for his existence
and in waging a continual warfare against both
animals and the elements the Indian gradually
formed a mythological category, personified and
humanised by him, which in time became his
all-absorbing thought and in fact the business
of his life, and this in turn was intensified by
his very nature which impelled him even more
forcibly along this line because of constant yearn-
ing for, and genuine love of war and supremacy.

The animals, plants, trees and rocks were regarded as human beings; the operations of nature
were looked upon as the magic performed by
various deities, such operations being ascribed
to the actions of divers magic powers. The
earth itself was considered as a person in both
form and body, every portion of which was
potent and filled with life, and this life was in
turn transmitted to those who lived or fed upon
her. The trees and plants were thus reckoned
as component parts because they received this
life-giving substance, and as such living beings
they were powers for either good or evil.
Prayers offered to them as gods were generally
beneficial unless defeated in turn by some higher
or more influential power.

As a giver of life to these trees, plants or other

products, the earth is almost universally regarded
with affection, and called Mother.   She produces
the many good things so needful to man and
creates as well the gods to whom he offers worship.
On the other hand this earth is likewise the taker
of life and she it is who devours the dead, *ergo* she
is regarded again as wicked and is debased.

All things that nature allowed to grow, from
the mightiest tree to the most insignificant
vegetable or weed, were of importance to the
savage mind, and were put in their place by
some all-powerful wizard; so too were the hills
and mountains similarly assigned and, unlike the
ethnic myths, this general conception was most
common.   The great and all-important principle
which underlies the mythology of the American
Indian is fundamentally the same principle which
dominates other and equally important groups
or bodies of mythologies, viz.: the principle of
transmigration or change through the exercise of
magic from one condition to another.

Among the Algonquian and Iroquoian of the
east the fire-dragon myth is both important and
of more than ordinary prominence, and among the
tribes of the Iroquois this dragon is also known
as the "light thrower."   In reality this is the
personification of the meteor, which flying

through the sky among the stars often appeared against a black background as some fiery serpent or reptile enveloped in flames. Further, they were believed to fly from one lake to another and were obliged, because of enchantment, to remain in their watery domain else the world would be set on fire. This same myth appears among the Ottawa and Chippewa, and the Iroquois and other eastern tribes have also the Thunder People comprising usually four mythical beings all of whom are staunch friends of mankind. This important myth is different in conception throughout the Lake regions and in the northern Mississippi and Missouri Valleys, also on the north-west coast of America as far as Alaska, where it is represented by the Thunder Bird.

Among the north-western Indians, notably the Haida, Tlingit and Tsimshian, the raven plays an important part as a creator, according to Boas, and this myth later spread to a considerable extent among the Columbia river peoples, gathering and assimilating in its progress.

Continuing eastward and within the borders of the United States, among the Nez Percés the coyote takes first place. His rôle is an unequal one however, combining that of hero, trickster and dupe and his many evolutions are most interesting to study. The coyote possesses magical powers and much cunning and through the aid of supernatural helpers he is often enabled to deliver his people from otherwise formidable monsters, or to deceive and outwit other animals perhaps his equals or superiors.

In spite of this he occasionally over-reaches himself, though he as often turns the tables and wins in the end. It frequently happens that he is greatly assisted by creatures originated by himself through his own magic and also through the power which is his of changing into some other form. As a trickster he disguises himself and wins wives. In the same way he steals food for Fox, his friend, and as a dupe he makes efforts to imitate the wiles of some other animals. Whatever his method of procedure he ranks first and foremost among this particular tribe as their hero *par excellence*.

Passing still farther toward the east the great Algonquian family becomes most prominent, and their chief culture hero and benefactor Nanabozho (Manabozho, Nenabozho) forms the leading character in an extensive cycle of myths, in which his exploits and numerous adventures are related in detail. Until recently this character was wholly misconceived, in fact it was the erroneous notion concerning this hero that gave birth to the "Great Spirit" idea which was thought to prevail among the Indians.

Among the Iroquois great stress is laid on the tree myth, which appears not only in their history but in their folk beliefs and decorative art as well as in their mythology proper.

The deeds of Nanabozho, or in fact of the mythical deities of other families, cannot be detailed at length. A paucity of data referring to the subject is the difficulty as concerns many tribes, while others again have been very fully dealt with. Dr Matthews has written exhaustively of the Navaho, Miss Alice Fletcher, than whom none other is better informed, has explained much concerning the Omaha, and Mr F. H. Cushing recorded the Zuni myths in a manner not to be excelled. Others have written on the subject as Dixon on the Maidu, Spinden on the Nez Percé and Dr Boas and Curtin on the north-western tribes, while Mr C. G. Leland dealt with the New England Indians in a similar manner. In the course of a short and necessarily concise account of this kind mere references only can be made to some of the more fundamental principles. It might be well, however, to offer a few words as to the Indians of the Plains among whom the deluge myth is almost universal.

This generally takes the form of a submerged earth restored, the act having been performed by beings partly if not wholly human, who procure information as to the material world through the efforts of a bird or diving animal. After knowledge was obtained as to the condition of affairs, the world became peopled somewhat after the manner previously described.

Animal tales are common and of course, as would seem natural, the buffalo is a favourite character. He is seldom encountered in other areas for obvious reasons, but on the other hand the beasts of the woodland tribes, such as the bear, beaver and elk, appear frequently among the folk of the Plains. Migration legends are also common.

The fascinating task of gradually working out the distribution of myths among the American aborigines is one that now occupies the students of American folklore, and as this study advances so will a clearer insight into the prehistoric culture among the tribes be obtained.

NOTES

Page 25. **Indian words.** It is difficult to convey to the Anglo-Saxon mind a clear understanding of the meaning of the spoken words of the American Indian. He has no written language and the dialects found from coast to coast may vary largely.

As an instance, the two Seneca-Iroquois words in the first paragraph on page 25, i.e., *ne'ogĕ*ⁿ', a synonym for deer, and *hadinioñgwai'iu'*, are indirect references to such an animal, and may serve as examples.

In the first word the accent is on the first syllable. The superior *n* makes the preceding vowel nasal; the apostrophe represents a glottal stop. In the second word the vowels *ai* have the value of *i* in the English *hide*, the apostrophe as before representing a glottal stop.

In the names of the gentes among the Iowa tribe of the Siouan family, also on page 25, each of the vowels has the Continental Latin value. In the first word *a*ⁿ and *i*ⁿ are nasalised vowels of this character; the *tc* in each of the several words stands for the sound *ch* in English *church*; the *x* in *Tcé-xi-ta* is a voiced sound corresponding to the unvoiced German *ch* in *acht*; the *Q* in *Qó-ta-tci* has the same value except that it is not voiced. The word *Pá-gça* is pronounced *Págtha*, the *ç* having the sound of the English *th* in *thin*.

As to the value of *ç* and *ch* as frequently used in Indian words through the volume, it is quite impossible to give any standard rule for the pronunciation, as in each instance the value must depend on the alphabet of the individual writer.

p. 42. **Labret.** The use of the labret is common among peoples of low culture, notably the negroes of parts of West Africa, the Eskimo of the Arctic regions, the Botocudo of Brazil, and certain of the Indian tribes of North America. It consists of a piece of wood, shell or stone varying in size and shape, sometimes long and conical, in which case it is inserted into the lip at one side. Sometimes flat disks are used, which are placed in perforations in either the upper or lower lip.

p. 47. **Venereal diseases.** There seems to be no positive proof that syphilis existed for any length of time before the white man reached America (Columbian or post-Columbian period). Signs of the malady are lacking from the older burials from Peru and other South American localities and examination of the skeletal remains of many tribes from the Mexican border to Alaska does not reveal traces of this easily communicable disease. In some cases the osteological collections are extensive and the examinations have been most thorough.

p. 72. **Catlinite** is known among the Indians and early travellers as "red pipestone." It is very handsome in appearance, varying from a pale to a dark reddish tint and consists of a fine grained argillaceous sediment which, when freshly quarried, is so soft as to be readily carved, and this was formerly done with stone knives and primitive stone drills. It is obtained from a quarry in south-west Minnesota and was first brought to the attention of mineralogists by George Catlin, the noted traveller and painter of Indian subjects, from whom it takes its name. An analysis made by Dr Charles F. Jackson, of Boston, is as follows:

Silica	..	..	..	48·20
Alumina	..	..	..	28·20
Ferric Oxide	..		..	5·0
Carbonate of Lime			..	2·60
Manganous Oxide			..	0·60
Magnesia	..	..	..	6·0
Water	..	..	..	8·40
Loss	..	..	..	1·0

p. 122. **Mescal.** This product, which consists of the fleshy leaf bases and trunk of various species of agave, must not be confused with the distilled spirit known in Mexico under the same name. It is a most valuable food resource among the Apache and among nearly all the tribes inhabiting the region producing the agave. So far as known it was not fermented among the Indians before the coming of the Spaniards.

BIBLIOGRAPHY

The bibliography of the subject is extensive, and in what follows no attempt is made to compile a complete list of works dealing with the American Indians. Those interested in pursuing the study will do well to turn to Professor Farrand's *Basis of American History*, where an excellent list of titles will be found, analytically arranged. The new *Encyclopædia Britannica* (11th edition) gives one of the best *résumés* available both from an anthropological and an ethnological point of view. Of first importance to the student are the publications of the Bureau of American Ethnology, comprising the *Annual Reports*, *Bulletins*, and *Contributions*, the last discontinued. These are veritable mines of information and cover nearly all phases of the subject.

Special monographs and reports are also to be found in the annual publications of the Smithsonian Institution and the National Museum, printed by the United States Government at Washington, and written by specialists of the first rank. The Pacific Railroad Reports, covering the early exploration of the western country, may also be consulted with profit.

Among American periodical literature may be mentioned the *Journal of American Ethnology and Archaeology*, which contains a vast amount of valuable material, and the *Journal of American Folklore*; the *Anthropological Series*, from the publications of the Field-Columbian Museum; *Papers*, *Memoirs*, and *Reports*, of the Peabody Institute; and the *Memoirs of the American Folklore Society*. *Anthropos*, and Petermann's *Mitteilungen*, published in Europe, also appeal to the American ethnologist. The series of *Memoirs*, published by the American Anthropological Association, are of the utmost importance and the *Journal*, issued by this Association (see below), is probably the greatest of all American publications of its character.

For a list of books almost covering the subject refer to Pilling's great contribution, *loc. cit.*, and the appendix to Hodge's *Handbook of American Indians*. The former is more extensive as it contains references to many manuscript sources, whereas Hodge's list purposely excludes titles not readily accessible to students.

The selection which follows contains only a few of the more important works, many of which are more comprehensive in scope than might be expected, but on the other hand essential to the study for that very reason. Numerous Proceedings and Publications of Institutes or Associations in America might also be cited in addition to those above, but the list must not be made too extensive here. The books marked thus * are especially recommended for those beginning a course of reading on the American Indians.

*ADAIR, JOHN.   History of the American Indians.   1775.

ALLEN, J. A.   The Geographical Distribution of North American Animals.   1892.

—— History of the American Bison.   1877.

*American Anthropologist, The.   Organ of the American Anthropological Association. (First and second series.)   1888 to date.

*BANCROFT, H. H.   The Native Races of the Pacific States.   5 volumes.   1874–1882.

BOLLER, H. A.   Among the Indians.   Eight Years in the Far West, 1858–1866.   1868.

BOURKE, J. G.   The Snake Dance of the Moquis.   1884.

BRIGHAM, A. P. Geographic Influences in American History. 1903.

BRINTON, D. G. American Hero Myths. 1882.

*—— The American Race. 1891.

*—— Myths of the New World. 1868.

*CATLIN, GEORGE. Illustrations of the Manners, Customs, and Condition of the North American Indians. 2 volumes. 1866.

—— O-kee-pa. A Religious Ceremony; and other Customs of the Mandans. 1867.

*CHITTENDEN, H. M. The American Fur Trade of the Far West. 3 volumes. 1902.

*CLARK, W. P. The Indian Sign Language. 1885.

COLDEN, CADWALLADER. The History of the Five Indian Nations of Canada. 1747.

CRANTZ, DAVID. History of Greenland. 2 volumes. (2nd edition.) 1820.

*CURTIN, JEREMIAH. Creation Myths of Primitive America. 1898.

DENIKER, J. The Races of Man. An Outline of Anthropology and Ethnology. (2nd edition.) 1900.

*DORSEY, G. A. Indians of the South-west. 1903.

DRAKE, S. G. Aboriginal Races of North America. 1860.

DUCKWORTH, W. L. H. Prehistoric Man. 1912.

*FARRAND, LIVINGSTON. Basis of American History, 1500–1900. 1906.

FEWKES, J. W. "Dolls of the Tusayan Indians." International Archiv für Ethnologie, Volume VII. 1894.

FIGUIER, LOUIS. The Human Race. 1872.

—— Primitive Man. 1870.

*FULTON, A. R. The Red Men of Iowa. 1882.

*GODDARD, P. E. Indians of the South-west. 1913.

GREGG, JOSIAH. Commerce of the Prairies. 2 volumes. 1845.

GRINNELL, G. B. Blackfoot Lodge Tales. 1903.

*—— The Indians of To-day. 1911.

*—— Pawnee Hero Stories and Folk Tales. 1893.

*—— The Story of the Indian. 1896.

HADDON, A. C. History of Anthropology. 1910.

—— The Races of Man and their Distribution. 1909.

—— The Study of Man. 1898.

*—— The Wanderings of Peoples. 1911.

HALE, HORATIO. Iroquois Book of Rites. 1883.

*HODGE, F. W. Editor. Handbook of American Indians North of Mexico. 2 volumes. 1907–10.

HORNADAY, W. T. The American Natural History. 1904.

—— The Extermination of the American Bison. 1887.

HOUGH, WALTER. The Hopi. 1915.

—— The Moki Snake Dance. 1901.

*Indian, The. The North-west, 1600–1900. The Red Man, The War Man, The White Man. (Anon.) 1901.

*JAMES, G. W. Indian Basketry. 1913.

—— Indians of the Painted Desert Region. 1903.

KEANE, A. H. Ethnology. 1899.

—— Man Past and Present. 1899.

KRAUSE, A. Die Tlinkit Indianer. 1885.

LANG, ANDREW. Social Origins. 1903.

*LEWIS and CLARK. History of the Expedition under the Command of. (New edition, edited by Elliott Coues.) 4 volumes. 1893.

McCoy, Isaac.   History of the Baptist Indian Missions. 1840.

*McKenney, Thomas L. and Hall, James.   History of the Indian Tribes of North America.   3 volumes. 1837–44.

*McKenney, Thomas L.   Memoirs Official and Personal, with Sketches of Travel among the Northern and Southern Indians, embracing a War Excursion and Description of Scenes along the Western Borders. 2 volumes. 1846.

McLennan, J. F.   Primitive Marriage. 1865.

Marett, R. R.   Anthropology. 1912.

*Mason, O. T.   Aboriginal Indian Basketry. 1904.

——— The Origin of Invention. 1901.

——— Woman's Share in Primitive Culture. 1894.

*Matthews, Washington.   Ethnography and Philology of the Hidatsa Indians. 1877.

*——— Navaho Legends. 1897.

*Maximilian, Prince of Wied.   Travels in the Interior of North America.   Translated by H. E. Lloyd. 3 volumes and atlas of plates. 1843.

Miner, W. H.   The Iowa. 1911.

Moorehead, W. K.   Prehistoric Implements. 1900.

Morgan, Lewis H.   Ancient Society. 1878.

*——— The League of the Ho-dé-no-sau-nee, or Iroquois. (New edition.) 1904.

——— Systems of Consanguinity and Affinity of the Human Family. 1871.

*——— A Study of the Houses of the American Aborigines. 1880. (A revised edition of this work is to be found in Contributions to American Ethnology, Volume iv, 1881.)

BIBLIOGRAPHY 159

Murray, C. A. Travels in North America during the
Years 1834–5–6. 2 volumes. 1839.

*Navaho. An Ethnologic Dictionary of the Navaho
Language. 1910.

*—— A Vocabulary of the Navaho Language, Navaho-
English. 2 volumes. 1912.

Nordenskiold, Gustav. The Cliff Dwellers of the
Mesa Verde. 1894.

Ogg, F. A. The Opening of the Mississippi. 1904.

Owen, M. A. Folk-Lore of the Musquakie Indians of
North America. 1904.

*Parkman, Francis. The Discovery of the Great West.
1869.

*—— The Oregon Trail. Sketches of Prairie and
Rocky Mountain Life. 1900.

Paxson, F. L. The Last American Frontier. 1910.

*Payne, Edward John. History of the New World
called America. 2 volumes. 1892–99.

Petitot, E. Monographie des Déné-Dindjié. 1875.

*—— Traditions Indiennes du Canada Nord-Ouest.
1886.

Pike, Z. M. An Account of Expeditions to the Source
of the Mississippi. 1810.

*Pilling, J. C. Proof-Sheets of a Bibliography of the
Languages of the American Indians. 1885.

Quatrefages de Breau, A. de. The Human Species.
1890.

Rand, S. T. Legends of the Micmacs. 1894.

Rink, H. Tales and Traditions of the Eskimo. 1876.

Robinson, Doane. A History of the Dakota or Sioux
Indians. 1904.

Russell, Israel. Rivers of North America. 1898.

160   BIBLIOGRAPHY

SAGE, R. B.   Scenes in the Rocky Mountains, and in Oregon, California, New Mexico, Texas and the Grand Prairies. (2nd edition.) 1854.

*SCHOOLCRAFT, H. R.   Historical and Statistical Information Respecting the History, Condition, and Prospects of the Indian Tribes of the United States. 6 volumes. 1851–57.

SEMPLE, E. C.   American History and its Geographic Conditions. 1903.

SEVERANCE, F. A.   Old Trails on the Niagara Frontier. (2nd edition.) 1903.

SKINNER, A.   The Indians of Greater New York. 1915.

STENNETT, W. H.   A History of the Origin of the Place Names. 1908.

TEIT, J. A.   The Thompson River Indians. 1898.

TOPINARD, PAUL.   L'Homme dans la Nature. 1891.

*TYLOR, E. B.   Anthropology: An Introduction to the Study of Man and Civilization. 1881.

—— Primitive Culture. 2 volumes. 1871.

—— Researches into the Early History of Mankind and the Development of Civilization. (3rd edition.) 1878.

WAITZ, T.   Anthropologie der Naturvölker. Band III. Die Amerikaner. 1862.

WARREN, W. W.   History of the Ojibways. 1885.

*WINSOR, JUSTIN.   Editor. Narrative and Critical History of America. Volumes I and II. 1889.

*WISSLER, CLARK.   North American Indians of the Plains. 1912.

WRIGHT, C. D.   Editor. Report on Indians Taxed and not Taxed. 1894.

INDEX

adobe, used in building, 102
adultery, 30
agriculture among the Pawnee, 83
Aiuoves, Aioues (Iowa Indians), 69
Alabama (State), 6
Alaska, 4, 8, 15, 49, 50, 51, 147
Algonquian stock, 39, 43, 50, 52, 55, 58, 59, 64, 66, 80, 89, 146, 148; Cheyenne tribe of the, 51
Alleghany Mountains, human remains east of, 16
Allis, Rev. Samuel, 88
Ameghino, F., 15
America, Central, 1, 4; North, 1, 2, 6, 10, 18; North-western, 144; North-western coast of, 147; South, 1, 15
American Antiquarian Society, 17
André, Père Louis, 69, 71
animism, 138, 139
anthropoid apes, absence of, 9
Apache Indians, 109, 111, 112, 113, 116, 117, 118, 122, 123, 125, 131
Apache sub-tribes: Arivaipa, 112; Chiricahua, 112; Coyotero, 112; Faraone, 112; Gila, 112; Gileno, 112; Jicarilla, 112, 113, 114; Lipan, 112; Llanero, 112; Mescalero, 112, 115,

116; Mimbreno, 112; Mogollone, 112; Pinal, 112; Pinaleno, 112; Querecho, 112, 113; San Carlos, 115; Tonto, 112; White Mountain, 112, 115
ápachu, 112
Apalachicola river, 4
"Apane," i.e. Pawnee, 79
Appalachian system, 5, 6
approaching dance, 76
Arapaho Indians, 59
Arctic coastal section, 51
Arctic Ocean, 7, 143; as a drain, 3
Arikara Indians, villages of, 57
Arizona Apache, 116
Arizona (State), 8, 95, 108, 109, 113, 115, 129
Arkansas river, 3, 90
Arkansas (State), 92
arrow, game of, 74
arrows, poisoned, 123
Asia, north-eastern, 144
Astoria, Oregon, 59
Athabasca, Lake, 7
Athapascan family, 50, 80, 94, 109, 111, 112, 130, 131, 143
Atius Tirawa, 84
Atlantic States, 26
Atlantic tribes, 39, 42
Atounauea (Iowa Indians), 70
Authontontas (Oto Indians), 69
Ayavois (Iowa Indians), 69
Aztec people of Mexico, 95

90, 91, 92; Iowa Indians of the, 51; tribe, 43, 44, 54, 55, 56, 57, 59, 68, 80, 90, 92
Skidi Pawnee, 80
skin, colour of, in Indians, 20; odour of, in Indians, 21
smoking, 33
"soaring eagle" dance, 76
social status of Indians, 23
sorcery, 30
South Carolina (State), 90
South Dakota (State), 60
Spinden, H. J., 149
stocks or Indian families, 11
sun dance, 60, 64, 65, 66
surgery, practice of, 46
Sutaio Indians, 58, 65
Swanton, John R., 34, 45, 91

Taft, Prof. W. H., 48
Tanoan family, 94, 131
Taos, New Mexico, 95
tattooing, 42; among Pawnee, 87; among Apache, 119; among Mohave, 127
teeth in the Indian race, 21
ten Kate, H. F. C., 91
Teton (Sioux) Indians, 56
Texas, 93, 95, 109
thievery among Indians, 29
Thomas, Cyrus, 89, 91
throwing stick or racket, 75
Thunder Bird myth, 147; People myth, 147
Tigua country, 96; Indians, 109
Tiguex (Tigua, New Mexico), 96
Timucuan family, 1
tiswin, Apache beverage, 114
Tlingit Indians, 147
Tonti, Henri de, 79
totemical grouping, 28
totemism, 24
treaty, Cheyenne and United States, 1825, 60

trephining, 46
tribes, organisation of, 25, 26
tsay-dithl or throw sticks, 125
Tsimshian Indians, 147
tufa or volcanic rock, used by Pueblo Indians, 101
tumuli, 72
"Turk, the," 79
Tusayan, 96

Uintah Mountains, 6
United States, 2, 5, 7, 9, 81; physiography, 2; coastal formation, 2; drainage system, 3; Indian Office, 91
Utah (State), 7, 93, 129
Ute Indians, 114, 134

"Valley, the"—see Virginia, the valley of
Vaqueros (Apache?), 113
venereal diseases, 47
Virginia, as New England, 3; (State), 90; the valley of, 6, 17
volcanoes in Mexico, 8; in Alaska, 8

wâbĕnō', 45
Wakonda, 43
Wapello county, Iowa, 72
warriors' dance (Eh-Ros-Ka), 76
warrior societies among the Cheyenne, 61; among the Pawnee, 85
war song (wa-sissica), 76, 77
Wasatch Mountains, 6
Washington (State), 5, 8
wa-sissica (war song), 76
waterways, system of, 4
Waw-non-que-skoon-a, an Iowa Indian, 68, 71
welcome dance, 75
Westermarck, E., 38

For EU product safety concerns, contact us at Calle de José Abascal, 56–1°, 28003 Madrid, Spain or eugpsr@cambridge.org.

www.ingramcontent.com/pod-product-compliance
Ingram Content Group UK Ltd.
Pitfield, Milton Keynes, MK11 3LW, UK
UKHW020315140625
459647UK00018B/1889